Anonymous

Zion Hymn and Tune Book

For Use in the Church, Prayer-Meeting, School and Houselhold

Anonymous

Zion Hymn and Tune Book

For Use in the Church, Prayer-Meeting, School and Houselhold

ISBN/EAN: 9783337404659

Printed in Europe, USA, Canada, Australia, Japan

Cover: Foto ©Thomas Meinert / pixelio.de

More available books at **www.hansebooks.com**

ZION

HYMN AND TUNE BOOK:

FOR USE IN THE

CHURCH, PRAYER-MEETING,

SCHOOL AND HOUSEHOLD.

Compiled and arranged by

S. T. E.

CLEVELAND:
PUBLISHED BY S. BRAINARD & SONS.
1866.

NOTICE.

This collection of Hymns and Tunes comprises those in general use among the colored people, both at the North and South, and hence will doubtless prove acceptable to them, in both sections of the country. It is to be presumed that it may also be of service to the church at large, because of the many popular Revival Songs to be found therein.

The melodies are presented, as nearly as possible, in their original versions. Those which are designated thus: (✱*) are especially protected by the publishers' copyright, from appropriation by other book-makers, who will not be at liberty to use them without the express permission of their respective composers.*

THE COMPILER.

ZION

HYMN AND TUNE BOOK.

---

1. COME AND LET US SWEETLY JOIN.

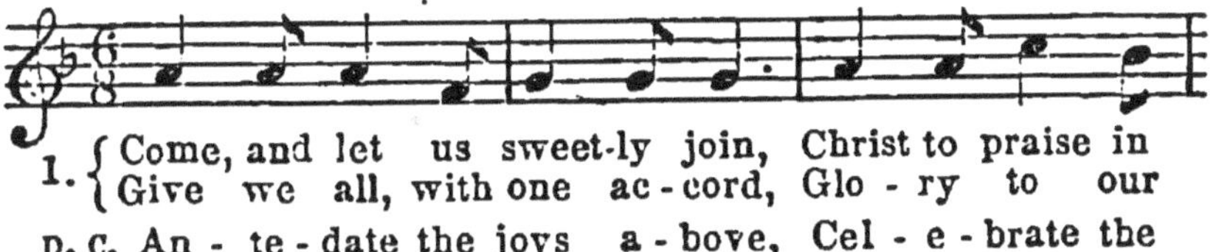
1. Come, and let us sweet-ly join, Christ to praise in
Give we all, with one ac-cord, Glo-ry to our
D. C. An-te-date the joys a-bove, Cel-e-brate the

Fine.
D. C.
hymns di-vine: Hands, and hearts, and voices raise;
com-mon Lord: Sing as in the an-cient days:
feast of love.

2. Strive we, in affection strive;
Let the purer flame revive;
Such as in the martyrs glow'd,
Dying champions for their God:
We like them may live and love;
Call'd we are their joys to prove;
Saved with them from future wrath;
Partners of like precious faith.

3. Sing we then in Jesus' Name,
Now as yesterday the same;
One in every time and place,
Full for all of truth and grace.
We for Christ, our Master, stand,
Lights in a benighted land:
We our dying Lord confess;
We are Jesus' witnesses.

4. Make us all in thee complete;
Make us all for glory meet;
Meet to appear before thy sight,
Partners with the saints in light.
Call, O call us each by name,
To the marriage of the Lamb:
Let us lean upon thy breast;
Love be there our endless feast.

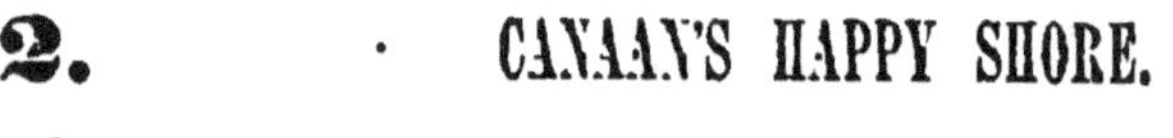

2. CANAAN'S HAPPY SHORE.

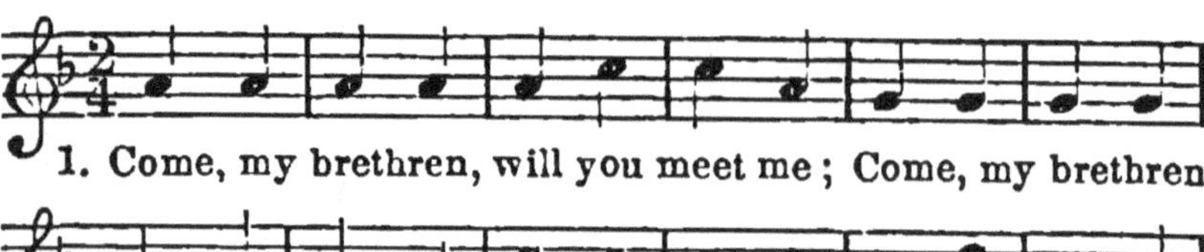
1. Come, my brethren, will you meet me; Come, my brethren,
will you meet me; Come, my brethren, will you meet me

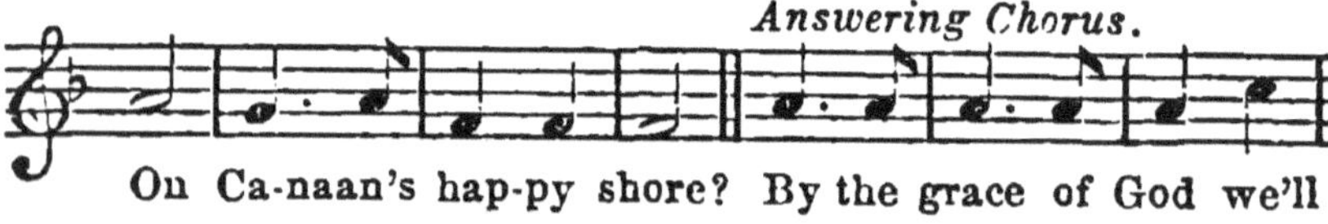
Answering Chorus.
On Ca-naan's hap-py shore? By the grace of God we'll
meet you; By the grace of God we'll meet you; By the

grace of God we'll meet you On Ca-naan's hap-py shore.

Full Chorus.
Then all hail, hal-le-lu-jah! All hail, hal-le-lu-jah!

All hail, hal-le-lu-jah! Je-sus comes to set us free.

CANAAN'S HAPPY SHORE. Concluded.

2. Come, my Sister, will you meet me,
   Come, my Sister, &c.

3. Come, our Leader, will you meet us,
   Come, our Leader, &c.

4. Come, Young Convert, will you meet us,
   Come, Young Convert, &c.

5. Come, our Pastor, will you meet us,
   Come, our Pastor, &c.

3. CHRISTIAN SOLDIER.

1. Hark! listen to the trum-pe-ters, They call for vo - lun-
teers; On Zi - on's bright and flowery mount, Behold their of - fi - cers: Their hors - es white, their
ar - mor bright, With courage hold their stand, Enlist - ed soldiers for their King, To march to Canaan's land.

2. It sets my heart all in a flame,
   A soldier now to be;
Oh, who'll enlist, gird on their arms
   And fight for liberty!

We want no cowards in our band,
Who will their colors fly;
We call on valiant-hearted men,
Who're not afraid to die.

3. To see our armies on parade,
How martial they appear;
All armed and drest in uniform,
They look like men of war.
They follow their great General,
The great, eternal Lamb—
His garments stained in his own blood,
King Jesus is his name.

4. The trumpets sound, the armies shout,
They drive the hosts of hell:
How dreadful is our God t' adore,
The great Emanuel!
Sinners, enlist with Jesus Christ,
Th' eternal Son of God:
And march with us to Canaan's land,
Beyond the swelling flood.

5. There on a green and flowery mount,
Where fruits immortal grow;
With angels all arrayed in white,
And our Redeemer know.
We'll shout and sing for evermore
In that eternal world;
While Satan and his army too,
Shall down to hell be hurled.

6. Lift up your heads, ye soldiers bold,
Redemption 's drawing nigh;
We soon shall hear the trumpet sound,
That shakes the earth and sky.
In fiery chariots we shall rise,
And leave the world on fire;
And all surround his glorious throne,
And join the heavenly choir.

4. OH, TURN YE.

1. Oh, turn ye, oh, turn ye, for why will ye die?

When God in great mercy is com - ing so nigh;
Since Je - sus in - vites you, the Spir - it says come,

And angels are waiting to welcome you home.

2. How vain the delusion that while you delay,
Your hearts may grow better by staying away;
Come wretched, come starving, come just as you be,
While streams of salvation are flowing so free.

3. And now Christ is ready your souls to receive,
Oh, how can you question, if you will believe;
If sin is your burden, why will you not come,
'Tis you he bids welcome; he bids you come home.

4. In riches, in pleasures, what can you obtain,
To soothe your affliction, or banish your pain?
To bear up your spirit when summoned to die,
Or waft you to mansions of glory on high.

5. Why will you be starving, and feeding on air?
There 's mercy in Jesus, enough and to spare;
If still you are doubting, make trial and see,
And prove that his mercy is boundless and free

6. Come give us your hand, and the Saviour your heart,
And, trusting in heaven, we never shall part;
Oh, how can we leave you? why will you not come?
We'll journey together, and soon be at home.

NO HOME HERE.

1. I would not live al - way; I ask not to

stay Where storm after storm rises dark o'er the way:

The few lu - rid mornings that dawn on us

here Are enough for life's joys, full e - nough for its

Chorus.

cheer. Home, home, sweet, sweet home, There's

no place on earth like my dear Saviour's home.

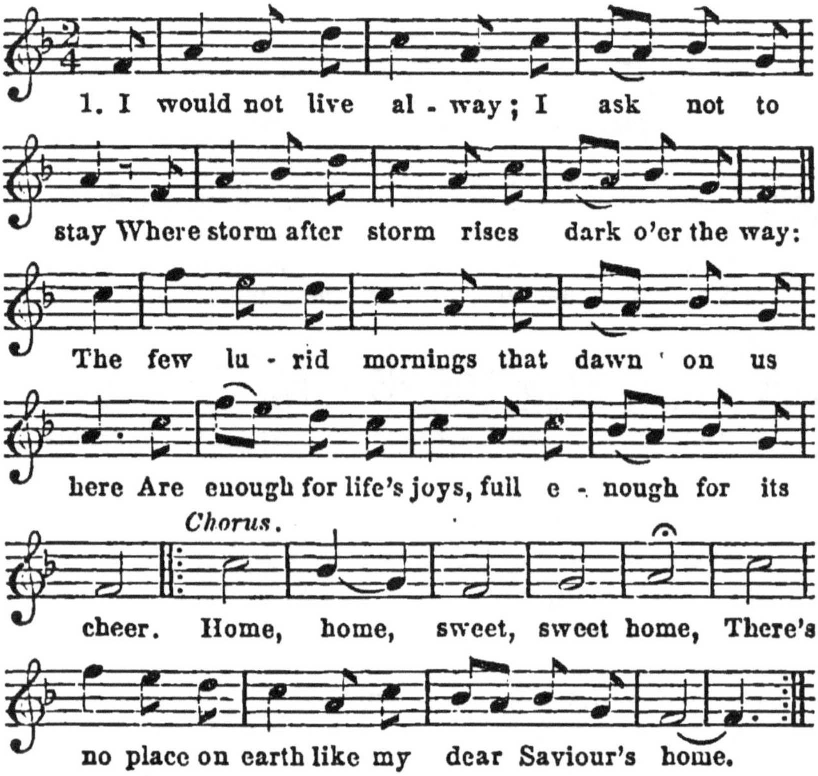

2. I would not live alway; no! welcome the tomb,
Since Jesus hath lain there, I dread not its gloom:
There sweet be my rest till he bid me arise,
To hail him in triumph descending the skies.
Home, home, sweet, &c.

3. Who, who would live alway, away from his God,
Away from yon heaven, that blissful abode,
Where rivers of pleasure flow bright o'er the plains
And the noontide of glory eternally reigns?
Home, home, sweet, &c.

4. There saints of all ages in harmony meet,
Their Saviour and brethren transported to greet;
While anthems of rapture unceasingly roll,
And the smile of the Lord is the feast of the soul.
Home, home, sweet, &c.

6. VICTORY.

1. Come ye that love the Lord in - deed, I'm
bound, I'm bound; Come ye from sin and
bon - dage freed, I'm bound for our home.

2. Great tribulation we shall meet, I'm bound, &c.
But soon we'll walk the golden street, I'm bound, &c.
3. Tho' hell may rage, and vent her spite, I'm bound, &c.
Yet Christ will save his heart's delight, I'm bound, &c.
4. Sound thro' the earth and down to hell, I'm bound, &c.
The powers of darkness can't prevail, I'm bound, &c.
5. Behold the righteous marching home, I'm bound, &c.
And all the angels bid them come, I'm bound, &c.
6. Ye everlasting gates, fly wide, I'm bound, &c.
For Christ awaits his coming bride, I'm bound, &c.
7. Ye harps of heaven, sound aloud, I'm bound, &c.
Here comes the purchase of his blood, I'm bound, &c.
8. There tears are gone, there sorrows flee, I'm bound, &c.
No more afflicted shall we be, I'm bound, &c.

7. ENTREATY.

*

1. Oh, brothers, be faith - ful, oh, brothers be faith - ful,
Oh, brothers be faithful, Till we all reach our home.

2. Oh, sisters, be faithful, &c.
Till we all reach our home.

3. There shall we see Jesus, &c.
When we all reach our home.

4. Then will we shout glory, &c.
When we all reach our home.

5. There 'll be no more parting, &c.
When we all reach our home.

8. REJOICE IN HOPE.

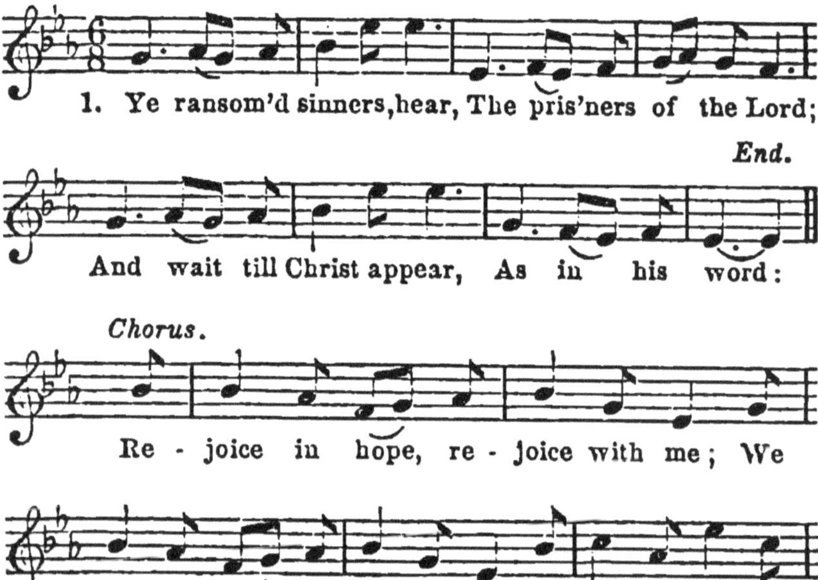
1. Ye ransom'd sinners, hear, The pris'ners of the Lord;
End.
And wait till Christ appear, As in his word:
Chorus.
Re - joice in hope, re - joice with me; We
shall from all our sins be free, Rejoice in hope, re-
D. C.
joice with me; We shall from all our sins be free.

2. In God we put our trust;
If we our sins confess,
Faithful is he and just,
He's righteousness.
To cleanse us all, both you and me:
We shall from all our sins be free.

3. Surely in us the hope
Of glory shall appear;
Sinners, your heads lift up,
Redemption 's near:
Again I say, Rejoice with me;
We shall from all our sins be free.

4. Who Jesus' suff'rings share,
My fellow-pris'ners now,
Ye soon the crown shall wear
On your pale brow:
Rejoice in hope, rejoice with me;
We shall from all our sins be free.

5. The word of God is sure,
And never can remove;
We shall in heart be pure,
And live in love:
Rejoice in hope, rejoice with me;
We shall from all our sins be free.

6. Then let us gladly bring
Our sacrifice of praise:
Let us give thanks and sing,—
Joy in his grace:
Rejoice in hope, rejoice with me;
We shall from all our sins be free

9. SINNER, WE ARE SENT.

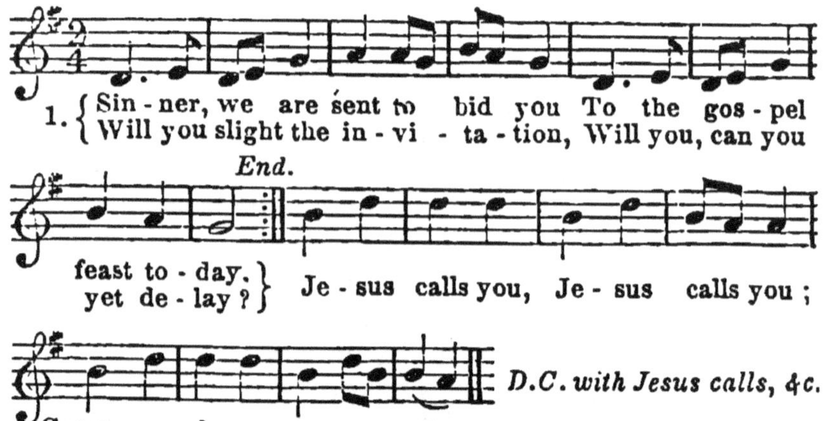
1. { Sin - ner, we are sent to bid you To the gos - pel
Will you slight the in - vi - ta - tion, Will you, can you
End.
feast to - day. } Je - sus calls you, Je - sus calls you;
yet de - lay ?
Come, poor sinner, come a - way.
D.C. with Jesus calls, &c.

2. Come, oh come! all things are ready,
   Bread to strengthen, wine to cheer:
If you spurn this blood-bought banquet,
   Sinners, can your soul appear
      Guests in heaven,
   Scorning heaven's rich bounty here?

3. Come, oh come! leave father, mother;
   To your Saviour's bosom fly:
Leave the worthless world behind you,
   Seek for pardon, or you die:
      "Pardon, Saviour!"
   Hear the sinking sinner cry.

4. Even now the Holy Spirit
   Moves upon some melting heart,
Pleads a bleeding Saviour's merit;
   Sinner, will you say, "Depart?"
      Wretched sinner,
   Can you bid your God depart?

5. What are all earth's dearest pleasures,
   Were they more than tongue can tell?
What are all its boasted treasures
   To a soul when sunk in hell?
      Treasure! pleasure!
   No such sounds are heard in hell.

10. EQUITY.

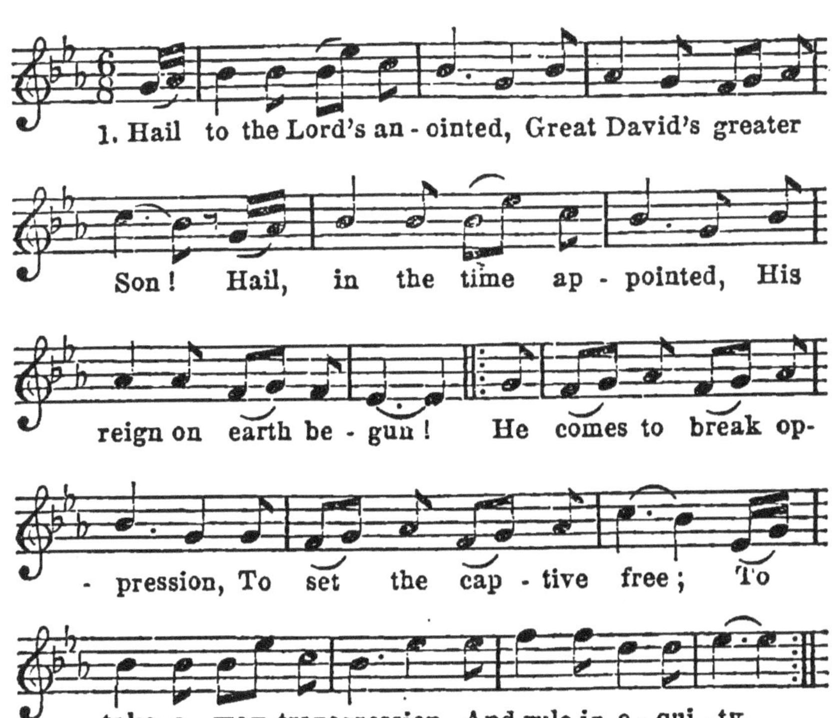
1. Hail to the Lord's an - ointed, Great David's greater
Son! Hail, in the time ap - pointed, His
reign on earth be - gun! He comes to break op-
- pression, To set the cap - tive free; To
take a - way transgression, And rule in e - qui - ty.

2. He comes with succor speedy
To those who suffer wrong;
To help the poor and needy,
And bid the weak be strong;
To give them songs for sighing,—
Their darkness turn to light,—
Whose souls, condemn'd and dying,
Were precious in his sight.

3. He shall descend like showers
Upon the fruitful earth,
And love and joy, like flowers,
Spring in his path to birth:
Before him, on the mountains,
Shall peace, the herald, go,
And righteousness, in fountains,
From hill to valley flow.

4. To him shall prayer unceasing,
   And daily vows ascend;
His kingdom still increasing,—
   A kingdom without end:
The tide of time shall never
   His covenant remove;
His name shall stand for ever;
   That name to us is Love.

11. OUR PASCHAL LAMB.

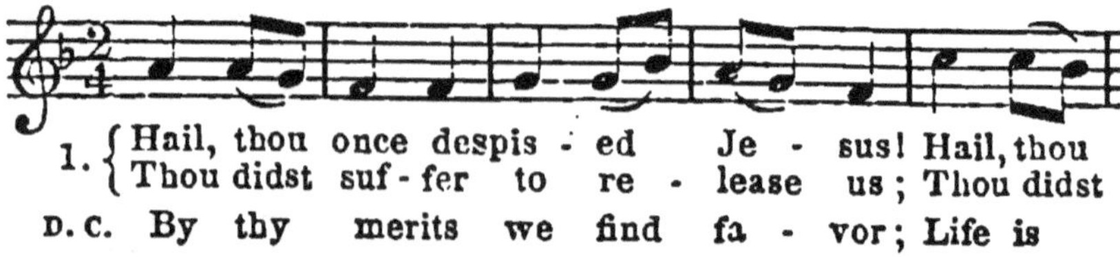
1. { Hail, thou once despis - ed Je - sus! Hail, thou
Thou didst suf - fer to re - lease us; Thou didst
D. C. By thy merits we find fa - vor; Life is

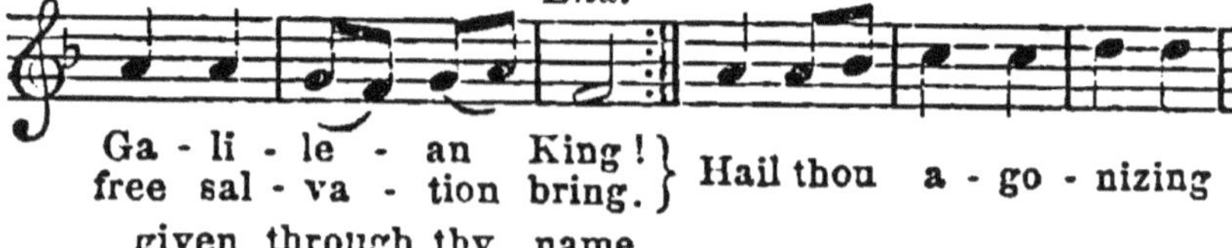
End.
Ga - li - le - an King! } Hail thou a - go - nizing
free sal - va - tion bring. }
given through thy name.

D. C.
Sa - viour, Bear - er of our sin and shame!

2. Paschal Lamb, by God appointed,
   All our sins on thee we laid:
By almighty love anointed,
   Thou hast full atonement made.
All thy people are forgiven,
   Through the virtue of thy blood;
Open'd is the gate of heaven;
   Peace is made 'twixt man and God.

3. Jesus, hail! enthroned in glory,
   There for ever to abide;
All the heavenly hosts adore thee,
   Seated at thy Father's side:
There for sinners thou art pleading;
   There thou dost our place prepare:
Ever for us interceding,
   Till in glory we appear.

4. Worship, honor, power and blessing,
   Thou art worthy to receive;
Loudest praises, without ceasing,
   Meet it is for us to give.
Help, ye bright angelic spirits;
   Bring your sweetest, noblest lays;
Help to sing our Saviour's merits;
   Help to chant Immanuel's praise.

12. I'M A PILGRIM.

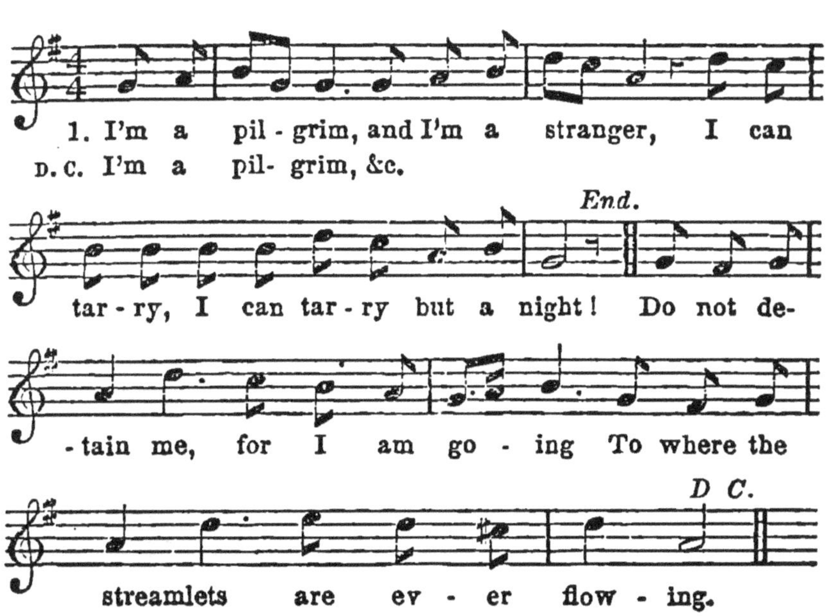
1. I'm a pil - grim, and I'm a stranger, I can
D. C. I'm a pil- grim, &c.
End.
tar - ry, I can tar - ry but a night! Do not de-
- tain me, for I am go - ing To where the
D C.
streamlets are ev - er flow - ing.

2. Of that city to which I journey,
My Redeemer, my Redeemer is the light;
There is no sorrow, nor any sighing,
Nor any tears, nor any dying.
I'm a pilgrim, &c.

3. There the sunbeams are ever shining,
Oh! my longing heart, my longing heart is there;
Here in this country, so dark and dreary,
I long have wander'd forlorn and weary.
I'm a pilgrim, &c.

4. Father, mother, and sister, brother,
If you will not journey with me, I must go;
For since your vain hope you still will cherish,
Should I, too, linger, and with you perish?
I'm a pilgrim, &c.

5. Farewell, neighbors, with tears I've warned you,
I must leave you, I must leave you and be gone;
With this your portion, your heart's desire,
Why will you perish in raging fire?
I'm a pilgrim, &c.

6. Farewell, dreary earth, by sin so blighted,
In immortal beauty soon you'll be arrayed;
For he who formed thee, will soon restore thee,
From sin and death to praise and glory.
I'm a pilgrim, &c.

13. THE UNIVERSAL KING. *

1. Young men and maidens, raise Your tuneful voices
high; Old men and children, praise The

Chorus.
Lord of earth and sky: Him three in one, and
one in three, Ex - tol to all e - ter - ni - ty.

2. The universal King
 Let all the world proclaim;
Let every creature sing
 His attributes and name;
Him three in one, and one in three,
Extol to all eternity.

3. In His great Name alone
 All excellences meet,
Who sits upon the throne,
 And shall forever sit:
Him three in one, and one in three,
Extol to all eternity.

4. Glory to God belongs;
 Glory to God be given,
Above the noblest songs,
 Of all in earth and heaven:
Him three in one, and one in three,
Extol to all eternity.

14. JUST NOW.

1. Come to Je - sus, Come to Je - sus,
Come to Je - sus — *just now.*

JUST NOW. Concluded.

2. He will save you—*just now.*
3. He is able—*just now.*
4. He is willing—*just now.*
5. He is ready—*just now.*
6. I believe it—*just now.*
7. Can you doubt him—*just now.*
8. See him pleading—*just now.*
9. Lo, he saves you—*just now.*
10. Hallelujah—*Amen.*

15. JUBILEE.

1. Blow ye the trumpet, blow, The gladly - solemn

sound; Let all the nations know, To earth remotest bound,

The year of ju - bi - lee has come; Return, ye ransom'd

sinners, home, Return, ye ran - som'd sinners, home.

2. Jesus, our great High Priest,
Hath full atonement made:
Ye weary spirits, rest;
Ye mournful souls, be glad:
The year of jubilee is come;
Return, ye ransom'd sinners, home.

3. Extol the Lamb of God,—
The all-atoning Lamb;
Redemption in his blood
Throughout the world proclaim:
The year of jubilee is come;
Return, ye ransom'd sinners, home.

4. Ye slaves of sin and hell,
Your liberty receive,
And safe in Jesus dwell,
And blest in Jesus live:
The year of jubilee is come;
Return, ye ransom'd sinners, home.

5. Ye who have sold for naught
Your heritage above,
Shall have it back unbought,
The gift of Jesus' love:
The year of jubilee is come;
Return, ye ransom'd sinners, home.

6. The gospel trumpet hear,—
The news of heavenly grace;
And, saved from earth, appear
Before your Saviour's face.
The year of jubilee is come;
Return, ye ransom'd sinners, home

16. I HAVE SOME FRIENDS.

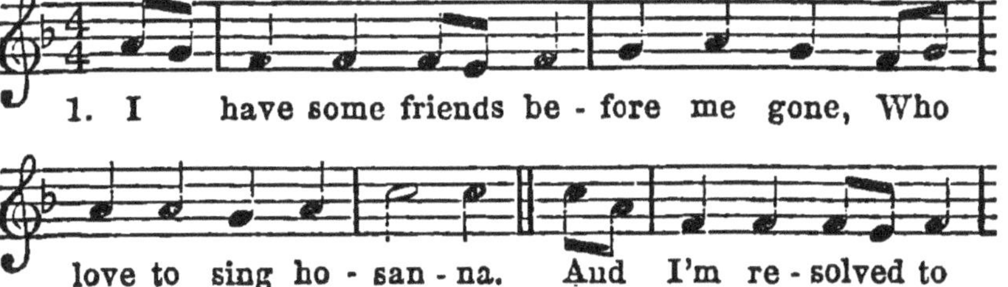
1. I have some friends be - fore me gone, Who
love to sing ho - san - na. And I'm re - solved to
Chorus. For we have but one more

Repeat for Chorus.
follow on, I love to sing ho - sanna.
stream to cross, And then we'll sing ho - sanna.

2. Ten thousand in their endless home,
All love to sing hosanna;
And we are to the margin come,
And love to sing hosanna. *Chorus.*

3. One family we dwell in him,
We love to sing hosanna;
Tho' now divided by the stream,
We love to sing hosanna. *Chorus.*

4. One army of the living God,
We love to sing hosanna;
Part of the host have crossed the flood,
Who love to sing hosanna. *Chorus.*

5. Amen, Amen, my soul replies, &c., &c.

17. LOVING KINDNESS.

1. Awake, my soul, in joyful lays, And sing the great Re-

-deemer's praise; He just - ly claims a song from thee, His
lov - ing - kind - ness, O how free! Loving - kindness,
lov - ing-kindness, His loving - kind - ness, O how free!

2. He saw me ruined in the fall,
Yet loved me, notwithstanding all;
He saved me from my lost estate;
His loving-kindness, O how great!

3. Though numerous hosts of mighty foes,
Though earth and hell, my way oppose,
He safely leads my soul along;
His loving-kindness, O how strong!

4. When trouble like a gloomy cloud,
Has gathered thick and thundered loud,
He near my soul has always stood,
His loving-kindness, O how good!

5. Often I feel my sinful heart
Prone from my Jesus to depart;
But though I have him oft forgot,
His loving-kindness changes not.

6. Soon shall I pass the gloomy vale,
Soon all my mortal powers must fail;
Oh, may my last expiring breath,
His loving-kindness sing in death.

7. Then let me mount, and soar away
To the bright world of endless day;
And sing, with rapture and surprise,
His loving-kindness in the skies.

18. COME, SINNERS.

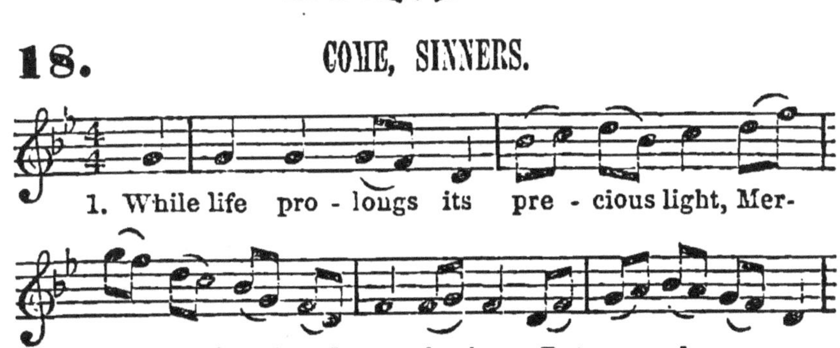
1. While life pro - longs its pre - cious light, Mer-
- cy is found, and peace is given; But soon, ah, soon, ap-

COME, SINNERS. Concluded.

- proaching night Shall blot out eve - ry hope of heaven.

Chorus.
While life pro - longs its precious light, Mer -

- cy is found and peace is given; But soon, ah, soon, ap-

- proaching night Shall blot out ev - ery hope of heaven.

2. While God invites, how blest the day!
   How sweet the Gospel's charming sound!
 Come, sinners, haste, O haste away,
   While yet a pard'ning God is found.

3. Soon, borne on time's most rapid wing,
   Shall death command you to the grave,—
 Before His bar your spirits bring,
   And none be found to hear or save.

4. In that lone land of deep despair,
   No Sabbath's heavenly light shall rise,—
 No God regard your bitter prayer,
   No Saviour call you to the skies.

5. Now God invites; how blest the day!
   How sweet the Gospel's charming sound!
 Come, sinners, haste, O haste away,
   While yet a pard'ning God is found.

19. OLD HUNDRED.

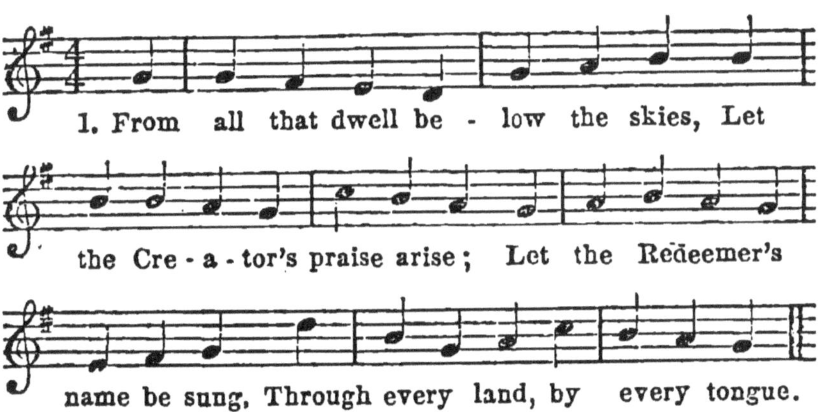
1. From all that dwell be - low the skies, Let
the Cre - a - tor's praise arise; Let the Redeemer's
name be sung, Through every land, by every tongue.

2. Eternal are thy mercies, Lord;
Eternal truth attends thy word:
Thy praise shall sound from shore to shore,
Till sun shall rise and set no more.

3. Your lofty themes, ye mortals, bring;
In songs of praise divinely sing;
The great salvation loud proclaim,
And shout for joy the Saviour's name.

4. In every land begin the song;
To every land the strains belong:
In cheerful sounds all voices raise,
And fill the world with loudest praise.

20. WE'LL MARCH AROUND JERUSALEM.

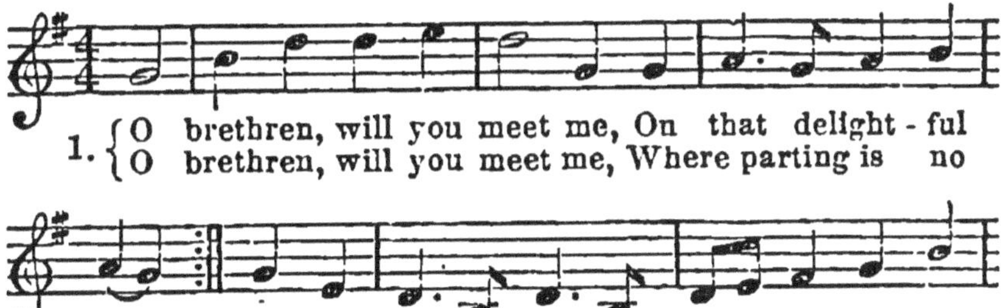
1. { O brethren, will you meet me, On that delight - ful shore?
O brethren, will you meet me, Where parting is no more? }
And we'll march around Je - ru - salem, We'll

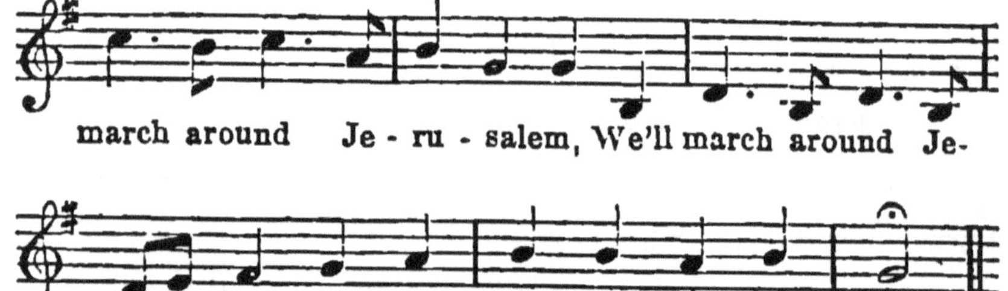
march around Je - ru - salem, We'll march around Je-
-ru . sa - lem, When we ar - rive at home.

2. O Sister, will you meet me, &c.
3. O Leader, will you meet me, &c.
4. O Preacher, will you meet me, &c.
5. Young Convert, will you meet me, &c
6. Yes, bless the Lord, I'll meet you, &c.
6. Backslider, will you meet me, &c.
8. O Sinner, will you meet me, &c.

21. GOLDEN HILL.

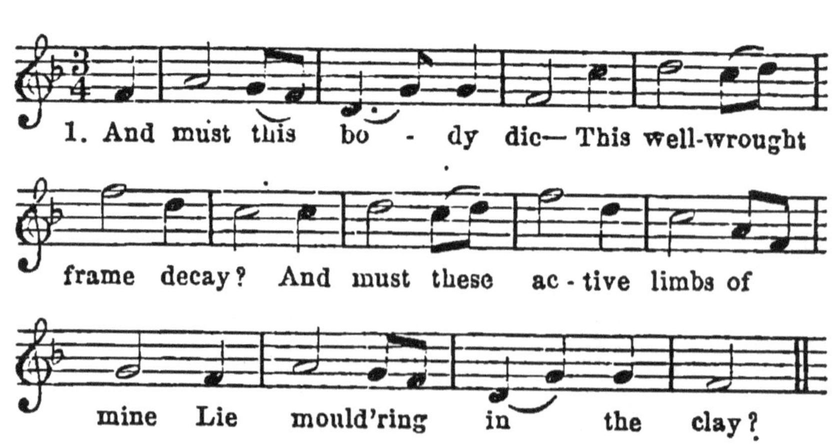
1. And must this bo - dy die— This well-wrought
frame decay? And must these ac - tive limbs of
mine Lie mould'ring in the clay?

2. Corruption, earth, and worms
Shall but refine this flesh,
Till my triumphant spirit comes
To put it on afresh.

3. God my Redeemer lives,
 And ever from the skies
Looks down and watches all my dust,
 Till he shall bid it rise.

4. Array'd in glorious grace
 Shall these vile bodies shine,
And every shape, and every face,
 Be heavenly and divine.

5. These lively hopes we owe,
 Lord, to thy dying love:
O may we bless thy grace below,
 And sing thy grace above!

6. Saviour, accept the praise
 Of these our humble songs,
Till tunes of nobler sound we raise
 With our immortal tongues.

---

22. I'M A TRAVELER.

1. I'm a lone - ly traveler here, Weary, oppressed;
For my journey's end is near—Soon I shall rest.

2. Dark and dreary is the way,
 Toiling I've come—
Ask me not with you to stay—
 Yonder's my home.

3. I'm a weary traveler here,
 I must go on,
For my journey's end is near—
 I must be gone.

4. Brighter joys than earth can give
Win me away;
Pleasures that forever live—
I can not stay.

5. I'm a traveler to a land
Where all is fair;
Where is seen no broken band—
All, all are there.

6. Where no tear shall ever fall,
Nor heart be sad;
Where the glory is for all,
And all are glad.

7. I'm a traveler, and I go
Where all is fair;
Farewell all I've loved below—
I must be there.

23. FROM GREENLAND'S ICY MOUNTAINS.

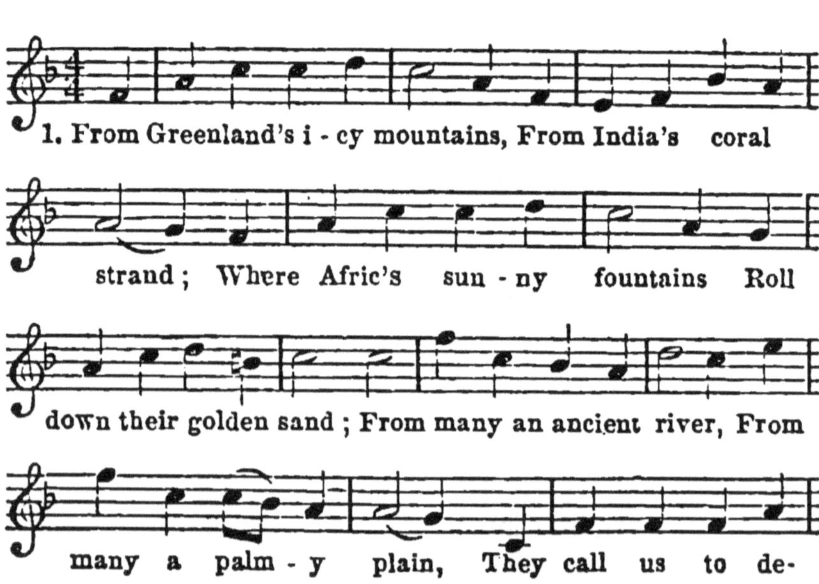
1. From Greenland's i - cy mountains, From India's coral
strand; Where Afric's sun - ny fountains Roll
down their golden sand; From many an ancient river, From
many a palm - y plain, They call us to de-

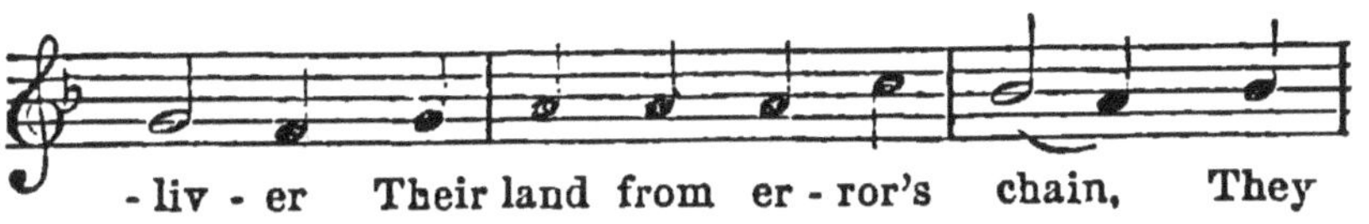
-liv - er Their land from er - ror's chain, They

call us to de - liv - er Their land from error's chain.

2. What though the spicy breezes
Blow soft o'er Ceylon's isle;
Though every prospect pleases
And only man is vile:
In vain with lavish kindness
The gifts of God are strown:
The heathen in his blindness
Bows down to wood and stone.

3. Shall we, whose souls are lighted
With wisdom from on high,
Shall we, to men benighted,
The lamp of life deny?
Salvation!—O salvation!
The joyful sound proclaim,
Till earth's remotest nation
Has learn'd Messiah's name.

4. Waft, waft, ye winds, his story,
And you, ye waters, roll,
Till, like a sea of glory,
It spreads from pole to pole:
Till o'er our ransom'd nature
The Lamb for sinners slain,
Redeemer, King, Creator,
In bliss return to reign.

24. OPEN THE GATES.

1. { Burst, ye emerald gates, and bring, To my raptured vision, }
{ All th' ecsta-tic joys that spring, Round the bright elysian. }

{ Lo, we lift our longing eyes, }
{ Break, ye interven-ing skies, } Open the gates of Paradise.
{ Sons of righteousness, a-rise, }

2. Floods of everlasting light,
Freely flash before him :
Myriads with supreme delight,
Instantly adore him ;
Angelic trumps resound his fame ;
Lutes of lucid gold proclaim
All the music of his name ;
Heaven echoing the theme.

3. Four and twenty elders rise
From their princely station ;
Shout his glorious victories,
Sing the great salvation ;
Cast their crowns before his throne,
Cry in reverential tone,
Glory be to God alone,
Holy ! Holy ! Holy One !

4. Hark ! the thrilling symphonies,
Seem, methinks, to seize us ;
Join we, too, the holy lays,
Jesus, Jesus, Jesus !
Sweetest sound in seraph's song,
Sweetest note on mortal tongue,
Sweetest carol ever sung,
Jesus, Jesus, flow along.

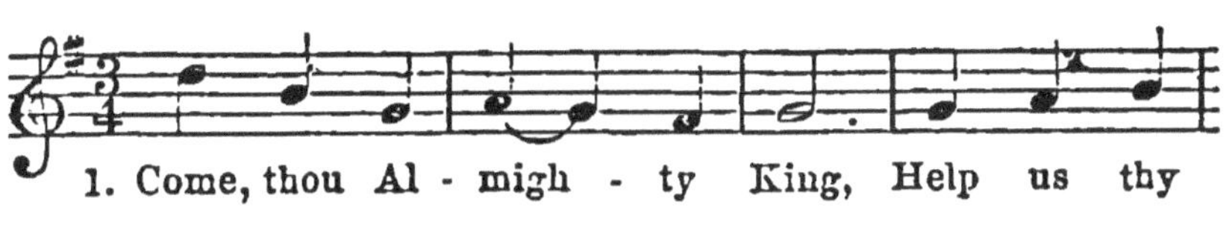
1. Come, thou Al - migh - ty King, Help us thy

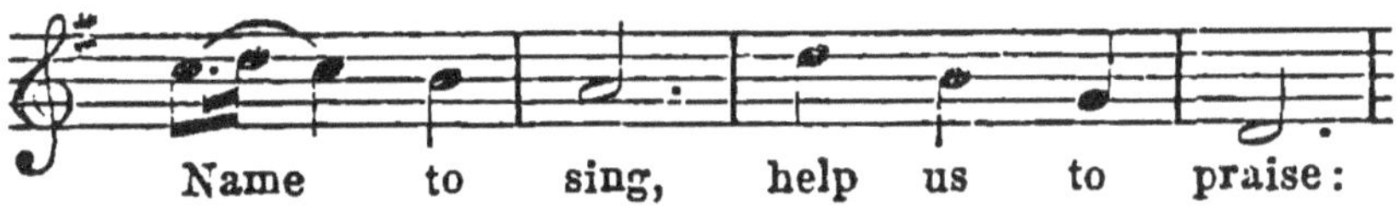
Name to sing, help us to praise:

Father all - glo - ri - ous, O'er all vic - to - ri - ous,

Come, and reign o - ver us, Ancient of days.

2. Jesus, our Lord, arise,
Scatter our enemies,
And make them fall;
Let thine almighty aid
Our sure defence be made;
Our souls on thee be stay'd;
Lord hear our call.

3. Come, thou incarnate Word,
Gird on thy mighty sword,
Our prayer attend;
Come, and thy people bless,
And give thy word success:
Spirit of holiness,
On us descend.

4. Come, holy Comforter,
Thy sacred witness bear
In this glad hour:
Thou who Almighty art,

Now rule in every heart,
And ne'er from us depart,
Spirit of power.

5. To the great One and Three
Eternal praises be
Hence, evermore.
His sov'reign majesty
May we in glory see,
And to eternity
Love and adore.

26. HAPPY LAND.

1. { There is a hap-py land, Far, far a-way—
Where saints in glo-ry stand, Bright, bright as day: }

Oh, how they sweetly sing, Worthy is our Saviour King;

Loud let his praises ring, For ev-er-more.

2. Come to this happy land,
Come, come away;
Why will you doubting stand?
Why still delay?
Oh, we shall happy be,
When, from sin and sorrow free,
Lord, we shall live with thee,
Blest evermore.

3. Bright, in that happy land,
Beams every eye;
Kept by a Father's hand,
Love can not die.
Oh, then, to glory run;
Be a crown and kingdom won;
And bright above the sun,
Reign evermore.

27. MY SAVIOUR.

1. My Sav - iour, my al - migh - ty Friend, When
I be - gin thy praise, Where will the grow - ing
numbers end,— The numbers of thy grace?
I trust in thy e - ter - nal word; Thy
goodness I a - dore: Send down thy grace, O
bless - ed Lord, That I may love thee more.

2. My feet shall travel all the length
   Of the celestial road;
And march, with courage in thy strength,
   To see the Lord my God.
Awake! awake, my tuneful powers,
   With this delightful song;
And entertain the darkest hours,
   Nor think the season long.

28. WORTHY THE LAMB. *

1. Come, let us join our cheer - ful songs With
an - gels round the throne: Ten thousand thou - sand
are their tongues, But all their joys are one.
Chorus.
Wor - thy the Lamb that died, they cry, To
be exalt - ed thus: Wor - thy the Lamb, our
hearts re - ply, For he was slain for us.

2. Jesus is worthy to receive
   Honor and power divine;
And blessings more than we can give,
   Be, Lord, forever thine.
      Chorus; Worthy, &c.

3. The whole creation join in one,
   To bless the sacred Name
Of Him that sits upon the throne,
   And to adore the Lamb.
      Chorus: Worthy, &c.

29. LAST CALL OF MERCY.

End.

1. { 'T is the last call of mer-cy, That lin - gers for thee.
   { Oh! sinner, receive it; To Je - sus now flee!

D. C. His offered sal - vation, And love is abused.

D. C.
He of - ten has called thee, But thou hast re - fused

2. If thou slightest this warning,
   Now offered at last,
Thine will be the sad mourning
   "The harvest is past,
Salvation I 've slighted,
   The summer is o'er,
And now there is pardon,
   Sweet pardon no more."

3. 'T is the last call of mercy,
   Oh, turn not away,
For now swiftly hasteth
   The dread vengeance day!

The Spirit invites you,
  And pleads with you, come!
Oh, come to life's waters,
  Nor thirstingly roam!

4. 'T is the last call of mercy,
  Oh, steel not thy heart,
For now she is rising,
  From earth to depart!
The last note is sounding
  The judgment is nigh
The Bridegroom is coming,
  Obey lest ye die.

5. 'T is the last call of mercy,
  That lingers for thee,
Break away from the bondage,
  Oh sinner, be free!
Be not a sad mourner,
  "The harvest is past,
The summer is ended,"
  And perish at last.

30. THERE IS A LAND OF PLEASURE.

1. { There is a land of pleasure, Where streams of joy for
'T is there I have my treasure, And there I hope to

1st time.
2d time.

ev - er roll;
[Omit - - - - -] rest my soul; Long darkness dwelt a-

-round me, With scarcely once a cheering ray; But
since my Saviour found me, A light has shone along my way.

2. I'm on my way to Canaan,
Still guided by my Saviour's hand;
Oh, come along, poor sinner,
And see Immanuel's happy land!
To all that stay behind me,
I bid a long, a last farewell!
Oh, come, or you'll repent
When you do reach the gates of hell!

3. The vale of tears surrounds me,
And Jordan's current rolls before;
Oh, how I stand and tremble,
To hear the dismal waters roar!
Whose hand shall then support me,
And keep my soul from sinking there;
From sinking down to darkness,
And to regions of despair?

4. The waves shall not affright me,
Although they're deeper than the grave
If Jesus will stand by me,
I 'll calmly ride o'er Jordan's wave.
His word has calmed the ocean;
His lamp has cheered the gloomy vale,
Oh, may this friend be with me,
When through the gates of death I sail!

5. Then come, thou king of terrors,
And with thy weapons lay me low:
I soon shall reach that region
Where everlasting pleasures flow.

Now, Christians, I must leave you
A few more days to suffer here:
Through grace I soon shall meet you—
My soul exults—I'm almost there.

6. Soon the archangel's trumpet
Shall shake the globe from pole to pole,
And all the wheels of nature
Shall in a moment cease to roll.
Then I shall see my Saviour.
With shining ranks of angels come,
To execute his vengeance,
And take his ransomed people home.

31. THE JOYOUS PROSPECT.

1. And let this fee - ble bo - dy fail, And
let it faint or die; My soul shall quit the
mournful vale, And soar to worlds on high;
Shall join the dis - em - bod - ied saints, And
find its long-sought rest, That on - ly bliss for
which it pants, In the Re - deem - er's breast.

2. In hope of that immortal crown
I now the cross sustain,
And gladly wander up and down,
And smile at toil and pain:
I suffer on my threescore years,
Till my deliv'rer come,
And wipe away his servant's tears,
And take his exile home.

3. O what hath Jesus bought for me!
Before my ravish'd eyes
Rivers of life divine I see,
And trees of Paradise:
I see a world of spirits bright,
Who taste the pleasures there;
They all are robed in spotless white,
And conqu'ring palms they bear.

4. O what are all my suff'rings here,
If, Lord, thou count me meet
With that enraptured host t' appear,
And worship at thy feet!
Give joy or grief, give ease or pain,
Take life or friends away,
But let me find them all again
In that eternal day.

32. MY COMFORTER. *

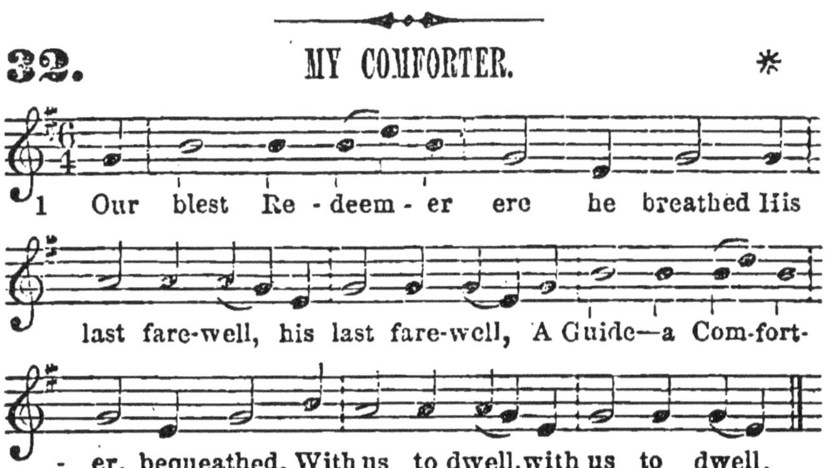
1 Our blest Re - deem - er ere he breathed His
last fare-well, his last fare-well, A Guide—a Com-fort-
- er, bequeathed, With us to dwell, with us to dwell.

2. He comes, his graces to impart;
 A willing guest, a willing guest,
While he can find one humble heart
 Wherein to rest, wherein to rest.

3. And all the good that we possess,
 His gift we own, his gift we own;
Yea, every thought of holiness,
 And vict'ry won, and vict'ry won.

4. Spirit of purity and grace,
 Our weakness see, our weakness see;
O make our hearts thy dwelling place,
 And worthier thee, and worthier thee.

33. HOW TEDIOUS.

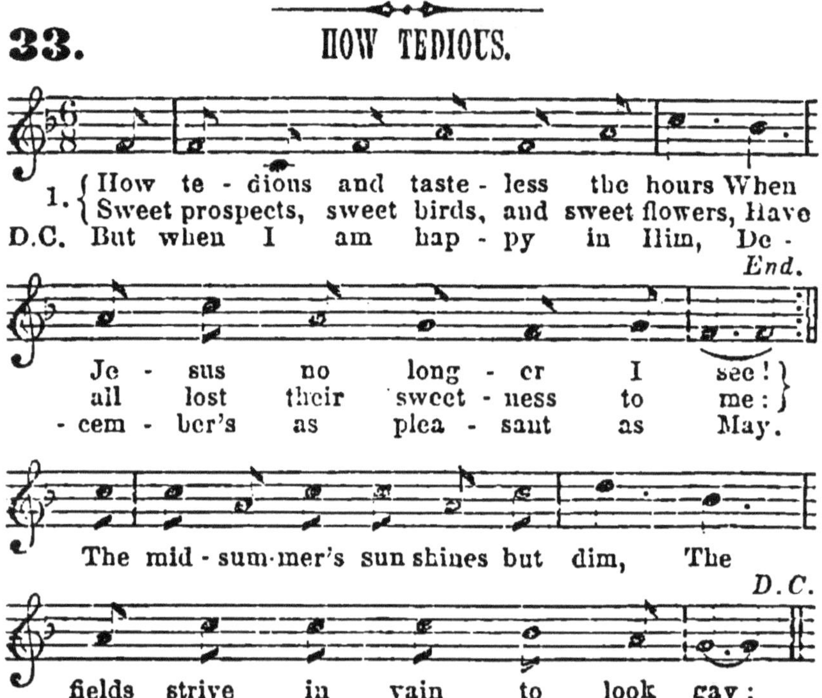
1. { How te - dious and taste - less the hours When
Sweet prospects, sweet birds, and sweet flowers, Have
D.C. But when I am hap - py in Him, De -
End.
Je - sus no long - er I see! }
all lost their sweet - ness to me: }
- cem - ber's as plea - sant as May.
The mid - sum-mer's sun shines but dim, The
D.C.
fields strive in vain to look gay:

2. His Name yields the richest perfume,
 And sweeter than music his voice;
His presence disperses my gloom,
 And makes all within me rejoice;

I should, were he always thus nigh,
  Have nothing to wish or to fear;
No mortal so happy as I,—
  My summer would last all the year.

3. Content with beholding his face
  My all to his pleasure resign'd,
No changes of season or place
  Would make any change in my mind:
While blest with a sense of his love,
  A palace a toy would appear;
And prisons would palaces prove,
  If Jesus would dwell with me there.

4. My Lord, if indeed I am thine,
  If thou art my sun and my song,
Say, why do I languish and pine?
  And why are my winters so long?
O drive these dark clouds from my sky,
  Thy soul-cheering presence restore;
Or take me to thee up on high,
  Where winter and clouds are no more.

34. COME ON, MY PARTNERS.

1. { Come on, my part - - ners in dis - tress, I
{ My com-rades through the wil - der - ness, I
have a home in glo - ry; } Chorus.
have a home in glo - ry; } O glo -
- ry! O glo - ry! There's room e - nough in

COME ON, MY PARTNERS. Concluded.

Par - a - dise, For all a home in glo - ry.

2. Beyond the bounds of time and space,
   We have a home in glory ;
   Look forward to that heavenly place,
   We have a home in glory.—*Chorus.*

3. Who suffer with our master here
   Shall have a home in glory ;
   And shall before his face appear,
   We have a home in glory.—*Chorus.*

4. Our conflicts here shall soon be past,
   We have a home in glory ;
   And you and I ascend at last,
   We have a home in glory.—*Chorus.*

35. YE SERVANTS OF GOD.

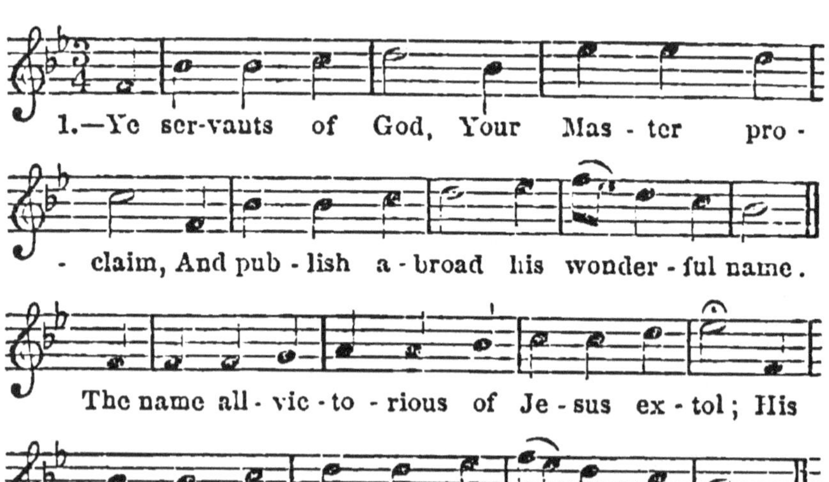
1.—Ye ser-vants of God, Your Mas - ter pro -
- claim, And pub - lish a - broad his wonder - ful name.
The name all - vic - to - rious of Je - sus ex - tol ; His
king - dom is glo - rious ; he rules o - ver all.

2. God ruleth on high, almighty to save;
And still he is nigh; his presence we have:
The great congregation his triumph shall sing,
Ascribing salvation to Jesus our King.

3. Salvation to God, who sits on the throne:
Let all cry aloud, and honor the Son;
The praises of Jesus the angels proclaim,
Fall down on their faces, and worship the Lamb.

4. Then let us adore, and give him his right,—
All glory and power, and wisdom and might,
All honor and blessing, with angels above,
And thanks never ceasing for infinite love.

36. OUR FATHER.

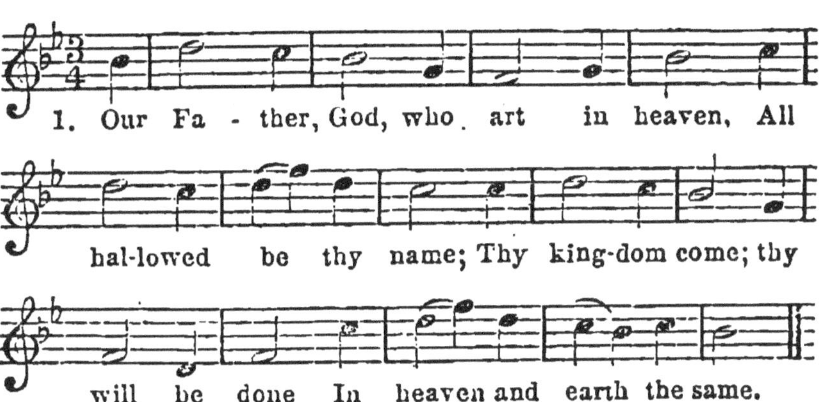
1. Our Fa - ther, God, who art in heaven, All
hal-lowed be thy name; Thy king-dom come; thy
will be done In heaven and earth the same.

2. Give us this day our daily bread;
And as we those forgive
Who sin against us, so may we
Forgiving grace receive.

3. Into temptation lead us not;
From evil set us free;
And thine the kingdom, thine the power,
And glory ever be.

 GLORY, HALLELUJAH! 

1. Thee to laud in songs di - vine Glory, Hal-le - lu - jah!

An - gels in thy presence join, Glory, Hal-le - lu - jah!

We with them our voi-ces raise, Glory, Hal-le - lu - jah!

Ech - o thine e - ter-nal praise, Glory, Hal-le - lu - jah!

2. Holy, holy, holy Lord,
Glory, Hallelujah!
Lord, by heaven and earth adored:
Glory, Hallelujah!
Thus, with them, we ever cry,
Glory, Hallelujah!
Glory be to God most high!
Glory, Hallelujah!

---

38. NOW THE SAVIOUR.

1. { Now the Saviour stands and pleading, At the sin-ner's
{ Now in heav'n he's in - ter - ceding, Un - der - tak - ing
D.C. Once he died for your be-hav-ior, Now he calls you

bolt - ed heart; }
sin - ner's part. } Sin - ner, can you hate the Saviour?
to his arms.

D.C
Can you thrust him from your arms?

2. Jesus stands, oh, how amazing!
   Stands and knocks at every door;
In his hand ten thousand blessings,
   Proffered to the wretched poor.

3. See him bleeding, dying, rising,
   To prepare you heavenly rest;
Listen, while he kindly calls you,
   Hear, and be for ever blest.

4. Now he has not come to judgment,
   To condemn your wretched race;
But to ransom ruined sinners,
   And display unbounded grace.

5. Will you plunge in endless darkness,
   There to bear eternal pain;
Or to realms of glorious brightness
   Rise, and with him ever reign.

40. O THOU.

1. O thou in whose pres - ence my soul takes de -
- light, On whom in af - flic - tion I call;
My com - fort by day, and my song in the
night, My hope, my sal - va - tion, my all.

O THOU. Concluded.

2. Oh, why should I wander an alien from thee,
Or cry in the desert for bread;
Thy foes will rejoice when my sorrows they see,
And smile at the tears I have shed.

3. Ye daughters of Zion, declare, have you seen,
The Star that on Israel shone?
Say, if in your tents my Beloved has been,
And where with his flock he has gone?

4. His voice as the sound of the dulcimer sweet,
Is heard through the shadow of death;
The cedars of Lebanon bow at his feet,
The air is perfumed with his breath.

5. His lips as a fountain of righteousness flow,
To water the gardens of grace;
From which their salvation the Gentiles shall know,
And bask in the smiles of his face.

6. He looks, and ten thousand of angels rejoice,
And myriads wait for his word;
He speaks, and eternity filled with his voice,
Re-echoes the praise of the Lord.

41. LOOK AT THE SOULS. *

Chorus.
1. Re-mem - ber what the Bi - ble says, Look at the souls
stand-ing at the bar! There's no re - pent - ance
in the grave, Look at the souls standing at the bar!

Hal - le - lu - jah to the Lamb! Look at the souls
stand-ing at the bar! Oh to stand on
God's right hand, That will be glo - ry.

2. See the gulf of black despair!
 Look at the souls standing at the bar!
Satan will torment them there,
 Look at the souls standing at the bar!—*Chorus.*

3. You will be forever damned
 Look at the souls standing at the bar!
If you spurn your heav'nly Friend,
 Look at the souls standing at the bar!—*Chorus.*

42. UNVEIL THY BOSOM.

1. Un - veil thy bo - som, faith - ful tomb; Take
this new trea - sure to thy trust; And
give these sa - cred re - lics room To
slum - ber in the si - lent dust.

2. Nor pain, nor grief, nor anxious fear
 Invade thy bounds: no mortal woes
Can reach the peaceful sleeper here,
 While angels watch the soft repose.

3. So Jesus slept;—God's dying Son
 Pass'd through the grave, and blest the bed;
Rest here, blest saint, till from his throne
 The morning break, and pierce the shade.

4. Break from his throne, illustrious morn;
 Attend, O earth! his sov'reign word
Restore thy trust—a glorious form—
 Call'd to ascend and meet the Lord.

43. HARK! FROM THE TOMBS.

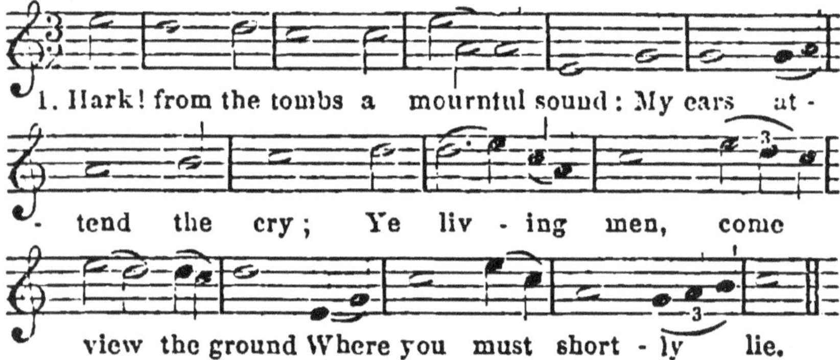
1. Hark! from the tombs a mournful sound: My ears at-
-tend the cry; Ye liv - ing men, come
view the ground Where you must short - ly lie.

2. Princes, this clay must be your bed,
 In spite of all your towers;
The tall, the wise, the reverend head,
 Shall lie as low as ours.

3. Great God! is this our certain doom,
 And are we still secure?
Still walking downward to the tomb,
 And yet prepared no more?

4. Grant us the power of quick'ning grace
 To fit our souls to fly;
Then, when we drop this dying flesh,
 We'll rise above the sky.

44. THE ROCK THAT IS HIGHER THAN I. 

1. In sea - sons of grief, to my God I'll re - pair,
When my heart is o'erwhelmed with sor - row and care,
From the ends of the earth un - to thee will I cry,
Lead me to the Rock that is high - er than I,
High-er than I, High - er than I,
Lead me to the Rock that is high - er than I.

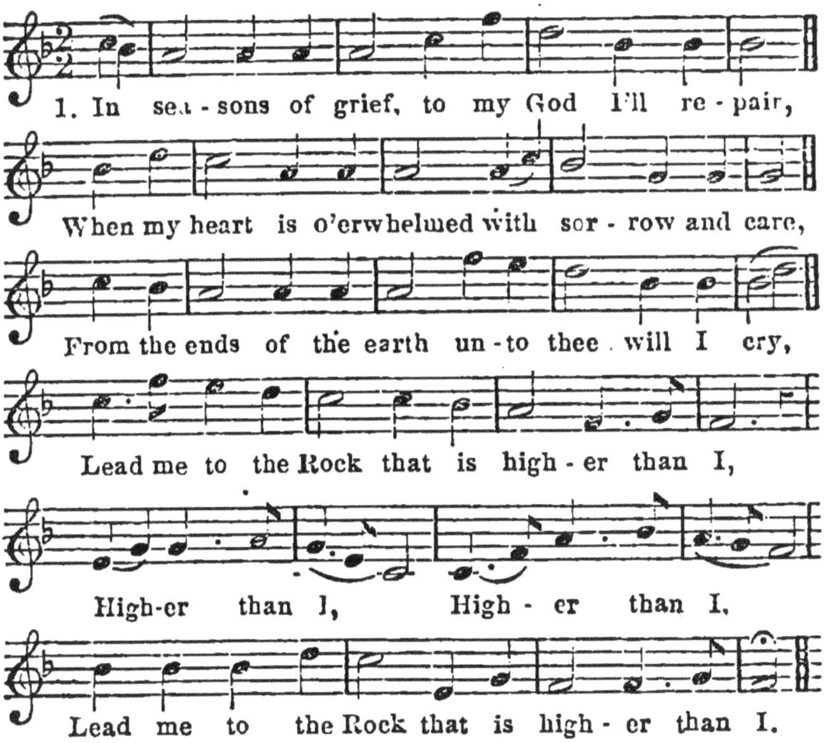

2. When Satan, the tempter, comes in like a flood,
To drive my poor soul from the fountain of good,
I'll pray to the Lord, who for sinners did die,—
Lead me to the Rock that is higher than I,
Higher than I, &c.

3. And when I have finished my pilgrimage here,
Complete in Christ's righteousness I shall appear,
In the swellings of Jordan all dangers defy,
And look to the Rock that is higher than I,
Higher than I, &c.

4. And when the last trumpet shall sound thro' the skies,
And the dead from the dust of the earth shall arise,
Transported I'll join with the ransomed on high,
To praise the great Rock that is higher than I!
Higher than I, higher than I,
To praise the great Rock that is higher than I.

45. SAY, BROTHERS.

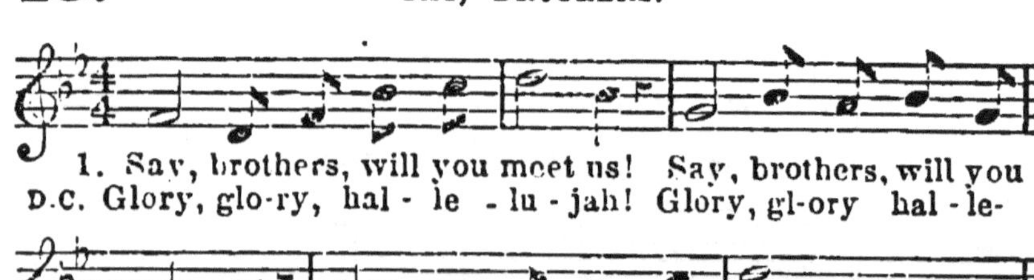
1. Say, brothers, will you meet us! Say, brothers, will you
D.C. Glory, glo-ry, hal - le - lu - jah! Glory, gl-ory hal - le-

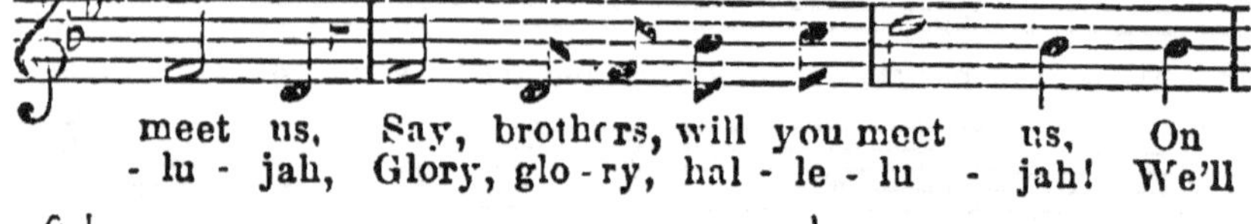
meet us, Say, brothers, will you meet us, On
- lu - jah, Glory, glo - ry, hal - le - lu - jah! We'll

Ca - naan's hap - py shore.
meet to part no more.

2. By the grace of Christ we'll meet you, &c.

3. Say, sisters, will you meet us, &c.

4. By the grace of Christ we'll meet you, &c

5. Oh, sinners, seek your pardon,
   And meet on Canaan's shore.

6. Yes, we will seek our pardon,
   And meet on Canaan's shore.

---

46. HEAR, O SINNER!

*

1. Hear, O sin - ner! mer - cy hails you, Now with sweetest
voice she calls, Bids you haste to seek the Sa-viour,
Ere the hand of just - ice falls; Trust in Je - sus;

HEAR, O SINNER. Concluded.

Trust in Je - sus; 'Tis the voice of mer - cy calls,
Trust in Je - sus; Trust in Je - sus;
'Tis the voice of mer - cy calls.

2. Haste, O sinner! to the Saviour—
   Seek his mercy while you may;
   Soon the day of grace is over;
   Soon your life will pass away!
   Haste to Jesus, haste to Jesus;
   You must perish, if you stay.

---

47. HAPPY DAY.

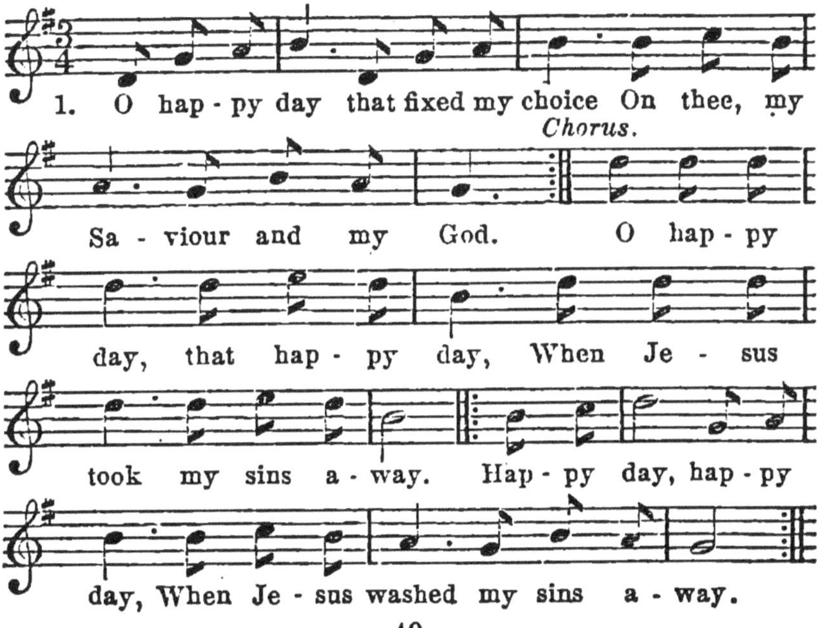

1. O hap - py day that fixed my choice On thee, my
Sa - viour and my God.

Chorus.

O hap - py
day, that hap - py day, When Je - sus
took my sins a - way. Hap - py day, hap - py
day, When Je - sus washed my sins a - way.

2. O happy bond, that seals my vows
To Him who merits all my love;
Let cheerful anthems fill his house,
While to that sacred shrine I move.

3. 'Tis done, the great transaction's done;
I am my Lord's, and he is mine;
He drew me, and I follow'd on,
Charm'd to confess the voice divine.

4. Now rest, my long-divided heart;
Fix'd on this blissful centre, rest;
Nor ever from thy Lord depart:
With him of every good possess'd.

5. High Heaven, that heard the solemn vow,
That vow renew'd shall daily hear,
Till in life's latest hour I bow,
And bless in death a bond so dear.

48. OUR BEST FRIEND. S. T. E. *

1. There's a Friend a - bove all others, Oh, how he loves!
His is love be-yond a brother's, Oh, how he loves!
Earth - ly friends may fail and leave us.
This day kind, the next de - ceive us,
But this Friend will never leave us, Oh, how he loves!

2. Blessed Jesus! wouldst thou know him?
Oh, how he loves!
Give thyself e'en this day to him,
Oh, how he loves!
Is it sin that pains and grieves thee,
Unbelief and trials tease thee?
Jesus can from all release thee,
Oh, how he loves.

3. All thy sins shall be forgiven,
Oh, how he loves!
Backward all thy foes be driven,
Oh, how he loves!
Best of blessings he'll provide thee,
Nought but good shall e'er betide thee,
Safe to glory he will guide thee.
Oh, how he loves!

4. Pause, my soul, adore and wonder,
Oh, how he loves!
Nought can cleave this love asunder,
Oh, how he loves!
Neither trial, nor temptation,
Doubt, nor fear, nor tribulation,
Can bereave us of salvation.
Oh, how he loves!

---

49. THE LOVE OF JESUS.

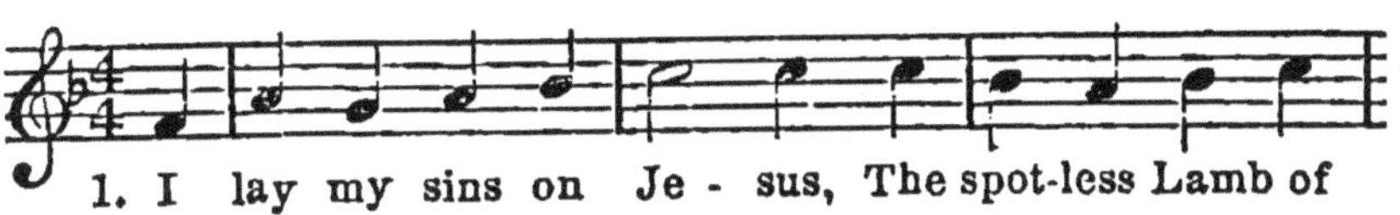
1. I lay my sins on Je - sus, The spot-less Lamb of

God; He bears them all, and frees us From

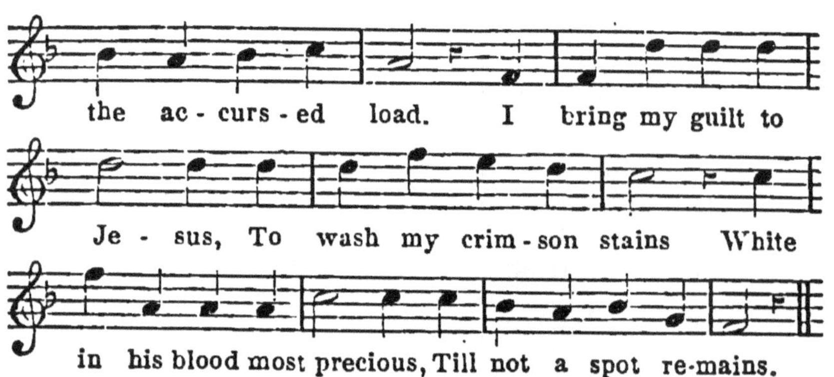
the ac - curs - ed load. I bring my guilt to
Je - sus, To wash my crim - son stains White
in his blood most precious, Till not a spot re-mains.

2. I lay my wants on Jesus,
All fulness dwells in him;
He healeth my diseases,
He doth my soul redeem.
I lay my griefs on Jesus,
My burdens and my cares;
He from them all releases,
He all my sorrows shares.

3. I long to be like Jesus,
Meek, loving, lowly, mild;
I long to be like Jesus,
The Father's holy child.
I long to be with Jesus,
Amid the heavenly throng,
To sing with saints his praises,
And learn the angels' song.

50. ALL HAIL.

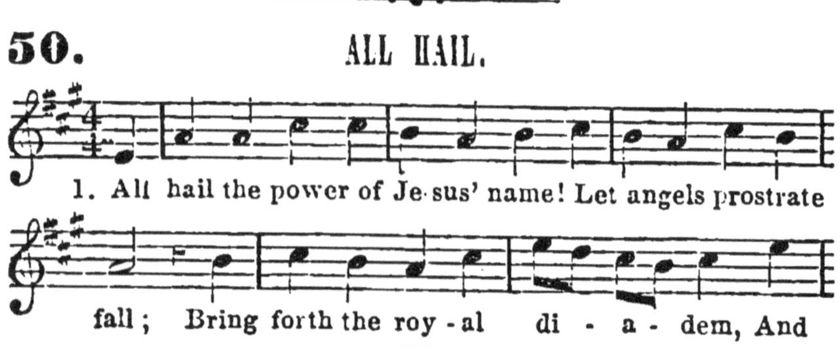
1. All hail the power of Je-sus' name! Let angels prostrate
fall; Bring forth the roy - al di - a - dem, And

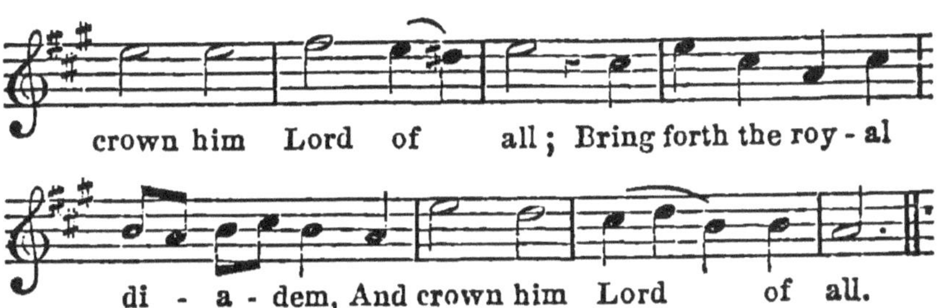
crown him Lord of all; Bring forth the roy - al
di - a - dem, And crown him Lord of all.

2. Ye chosen seed of Israel's race,
Ye ransomed from the fall;
Hail him who saves you by his grace,
And crown him Lord of all.

3. Sinners, whose love can ne'er forget
The wormwood and the gall;
Go, spread your trophies at his feet,
And crown him Lord of all,

4. Let every kindred, every tribe,
On this terrestrial ball,
To him all majesty ascribe,
And crown him Lord of all.

51. ON THE CROSS.

LESTA VESE.

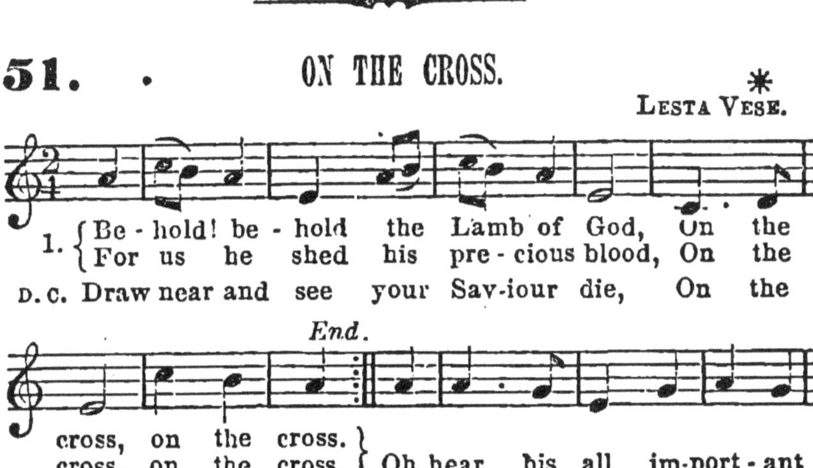
1. Be - hold! be - hold the Lamb of God, On the
For us he shed his pre - cious blood, On the
D.C. Draw near and see your Sav-iour die, On the
End.
cross, on the cross.
cross, on the cross. Oh hear his all im-port - ant
cross, on the cross.

D. C
cry, E - li, la - ma sa - bac - than - i—

2. Behold his arms extended wide
On the cross.
Behold his bleeding hands and side
On the cross.
The sun withholds its rays of light,
The heavens are clothed in shades of night,
While Jesus doth with devils fight,
On the cross.

3. Come, sinners, see him lifted up
On the cross.
For you he drinks the bitter cup
On the cross.
The rocks do rend, the mountains quake,
While Jesus doth atonement make,
While Jesus suffers for our sake,
On the cross.

4. And now the mighty deed is done
On the cross.
The battle's fought, the victory's won
On the cross.
To heaven he turns his languid eyes,
"'Tis finished!" now the conqueror cries,
Then bows his sacred head and dies,
On the cross.

---

53. NATIONAL HYMN.

1. God of eve - ry land and na - tion,

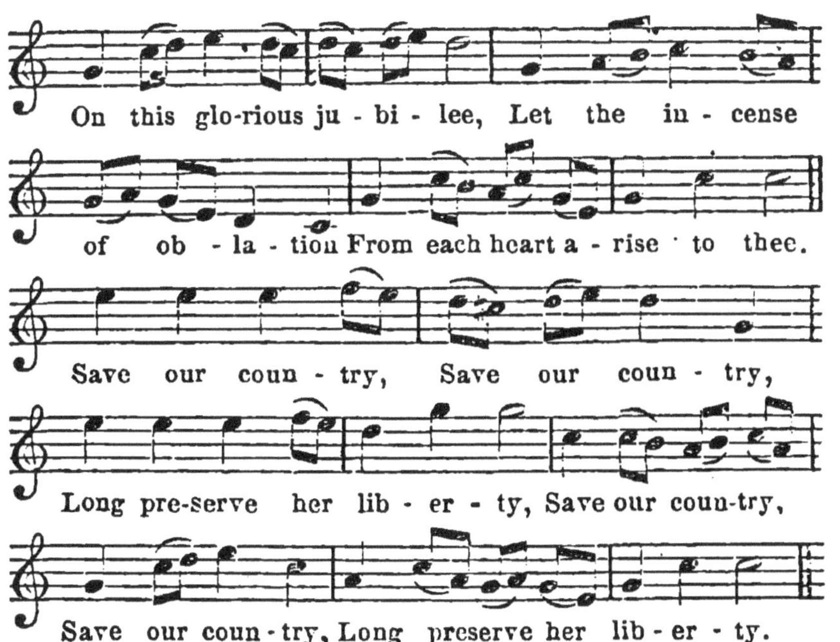
On this glo-rious ju - bi - lee, Let the in - cense
of ob - la - tion From each heart a - rise to thee.
Save our coun - try, Save our coun - try,
Long pre-serve her lib - er - ty, Save our coun-try,
Save our coun - try, Long preserve her lib - er - ty.

2. Let thy richest blessings ever
Rest upon our happy land;
May no fierce contention sever
Our beloved sister band;
In sweet union
May we still unshaken stand.

3. May we all be safely guided,
Saviour, by thy gracious will;
When life's storms shall have subsided,
And our tongues in death are still,
May we praise thee,
Where immortal glories thrill.

---

53. I HAVE A FATHER.

1. I have a Fa - ther in the prom - ised land,

I HAVE A FATHER. Concluded.

I have a Fa - ther in the prom - ised land,
My Fa - ther calls me I must go, To
Chorus.
meet him in the prom - ised land. I'll a
- way, I'll a - way to the prom- ised land, I'll a -
- way, I'll a - way to the prom - ised land,
My Fa - ther calls me, I must go, To
meet Him in the prom - ised - laud.

2. I have a Saviour in the promised land,
I have a Saviour in the promised land,
My Saviour calls me, I must go,
To meet Him in the promised land.
I 'll away, I 'llaway to the promised land,
I 'll away, I 'll away to the promised land,
My Saviour calls me, I must go,
To meet Him in the promised land.

3. I have a crown in the promised land,
I have a crown in the promised land,

I HAVE A FATHER. Concluded.

When Jesus calls me, I must go,
To wear it in the promised land,
I 'll away, I 'll away to the promised land,
I'll away, I'll away to the promised land,
When Jesus calls me, I must go,
To meet Him in the promised land.

---

54. OUR THEME.

1. Christ and his cross are all our theme, The
mysteries that we speak Are scan dal in the Jew's es -
Chorus.
steem, And fol - ly to the Greek. Oh you
must love the Sa - viour and your Lord, For you
can't go to hea - ven if you don't.

2. But souls enlightened from above
   With joy receive the word;
They see what wisdom, power, and love,
   Shine in their dying Lord.—*Chorus.*

3. The vital savor of His name
   Restores their fainting breath;
But unbelief perverts the same
   To guilt, despair, and death.—*Chorus.*

4. Till God diffuse his graces down,
Like showers of heavenly rain,
In vain Apollos sows the ground,
And Paul may plant in vain.—*Chorus.*

55. OH, 'TIS LOVE. *

Words by VARELIA. *By permission.*

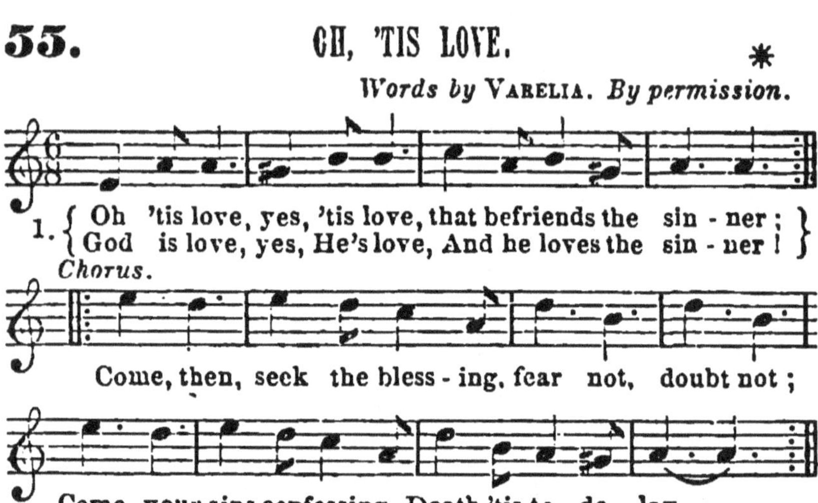
1. { Oh 'tis love, yes, 'tis love, that befriends the sin - ner ; }
{ God is love, yes, He's love, And he loves the sin - ner ! }
Chorus.
Come, then, seek the bless - ing, fear not, doubt not ;
Come, your sins confessing, Death 'tis to de - lay.

2. Jesus died, Jesus died,
Jesus died to save us ;
Now He waits, now He waits,
Waits but to be gracious.—*Chorus.*

3. Spurn ye not, spurn ye not,
Jesus' great salvation,
Or you'll meet, yes, you'll meet,
Jesus' condemnation.—*Chorus.*

56. LIVE IN LOVE. *

1. Moth - er, you live in love, Moth - er, you

LIVE IN LOVE. Concluded.

live in love, Moth - er, you live in love, To

Chorus.

glo - ri - fy the Lord. There's Cher - u - bim and

Se - ra-phim, An - gels, arch-an - gels, who bring the glad

tid - ings, Oh who are they that have

come out of great trib - u - la - tion, And

washed their robes in the blood of the Lamb.

2. Father, you live in love, &c.
3. Sister, you live in love, &c.
4. Brother, you live in love, &c

57. HOW HE SHOULDERS UP THE CROSS. *

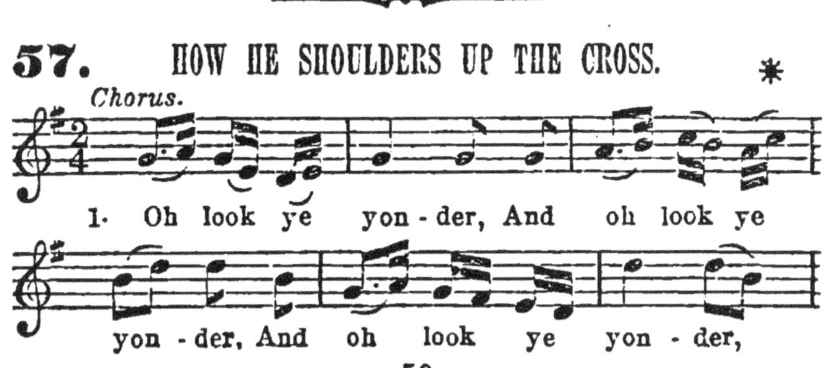
Chorus.
1. Oh look ye yon - der, And oh look ye
yon - der, And oh look ye yon - der,

End.
How He shoul - ders up the cross. It
was for you that Je - sus died, Oh look ye
you - der! For you that he was cru - ci - fied,
Oh look ye yon - der.
D.C.

2. Oh, see the cruel crown of thorns,
Oh, look ye yonder!
The wicked sinner Jesus scorns,
Oh, look ye yonder!—*Chorus.*

3. He's going to hang upon that cross,
Oh, look ye yonder!
Your precious gain is His great loss,
Oh, look ye yonder!—*Chorus.*

4. Soon they will nail his feet and hands,
Oh, look ye yonder!
His blood will flow for all the lands,
Oh, look ye yonder!—*Chorus.*

5. They'll pierce his side, Oh, wicked men!
Oh, look ye yonder!
Shall He have died for you in vain?
Oh, look ye yonder!—*Chorus.*

58. AWAY OVER YONDER.

Chorus.

Chorus.
1. A - way o - ver yon - der, way o - ver

yon - der, Way o - ver yon - der they

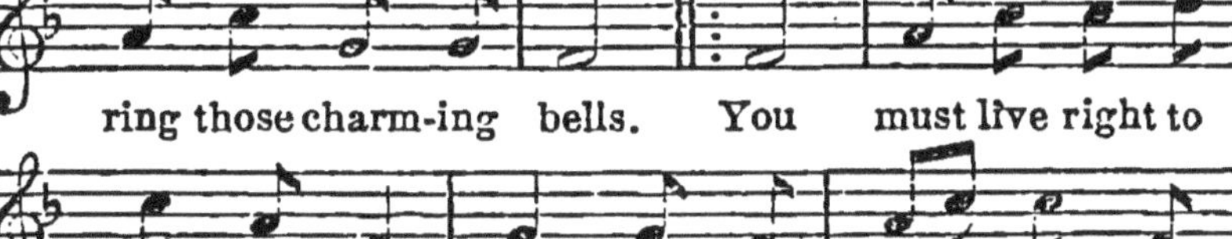
End.
ring those charm-ing bells. You must live right to

ring those bells, Way o - ver yon - der, You
D.C.

must live right to ring those bells, to ring those charming bells.

2. My mother has gone far away,
   Way over yonder;
My mother's been gone many a day,
To ring those charming bells.—*Chorus.*

3. You must pray right to ring those bells,
   Way over yonder;
You must live right to ring those bells,
To ring those charming bells.—*Chorus.*

4. Oh, listen to those charming bells,
   Way over yonder;
Dear Christians, you will soon be there,
And ring those charming bells.—*Chorus.*

---

59. I'M BOUND FOR THE LAND.

1. { To - geth - er let us sweet - ly live
To - geth - er let us sweet - ly die

I'M BOUND FOR THE LAND. Concluded.

I am bound for the land of Ca - naan;
I am bound for the land of Ca - naan.
O Ca - - naan, bright Ca - naan, I am
bound for the land of Ca - naan; O Canaan it is my
hap - py home, I am bound for the land of Can - aan.

2. If you get there before I do,
I am bound for the land of Canaan;
Then praise the Lord, I 'm coming too,
I am bound for the land of Canaan.
O Canaan, &c.

3. Part of my friends the prize have won,
I am bound for the land of Canaan;
And I 'm resolved to travel on,
I am bound for the land of Canaan.
O Canaan, &c.

4. Then come with me, beloved friend,
I am bound for the land of Canaan;
The joys of heaven shall never end.
I am bound for the land of Canaan.
O Canaan, &c.

5. Our songs of praise shall fill the skies,
I am bound for the land of Canaan.
While higher still our joys they rise,
I am bound for the land of Canaan.
O Canaan, &c.

60. THE OLD SHIP ZION.

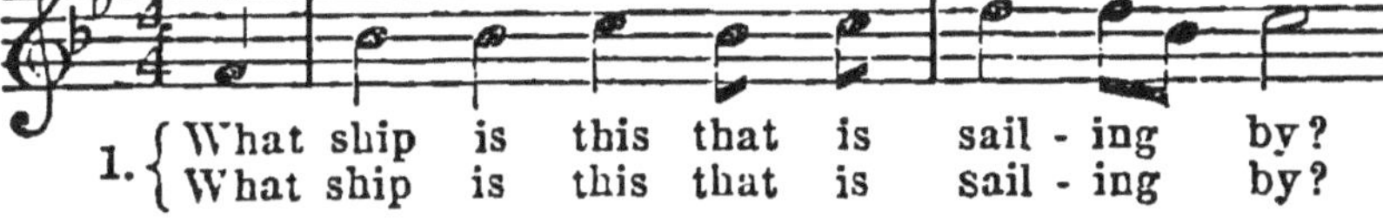
1. { What ship is this that is sail - ing by?
{ What ship is this that is sail - ing by?

O Glo - ry Hal - le - lu - jah! 'Tis the
O Glo - ry Hal - le - lu - jah! 'Tis the

old ship Zi - on, Hal - le - lu - jah,
old ship Zi - on, [OMIT - - -] Hal-le - lu - jah.

2. Pray tell me what is your captain's name?
'T is "the meek and lowly Jesus," Hallelujah, &c.

3. Is your ship well built, are her timbers all sound?
Why, she's built of gospel timber, Hallelujah, &c.

4. Do you think she 'll be able to face the storm?
Why she 's landed thousands over, Hallelujah, &c.

5. Oh what shall we do when we all get home?
We will sing and shout for ever, Hallelujah, &c.

6. What must a sinner do to be taken on board?
He must give himself to Jesus, Hallelujah, &c.

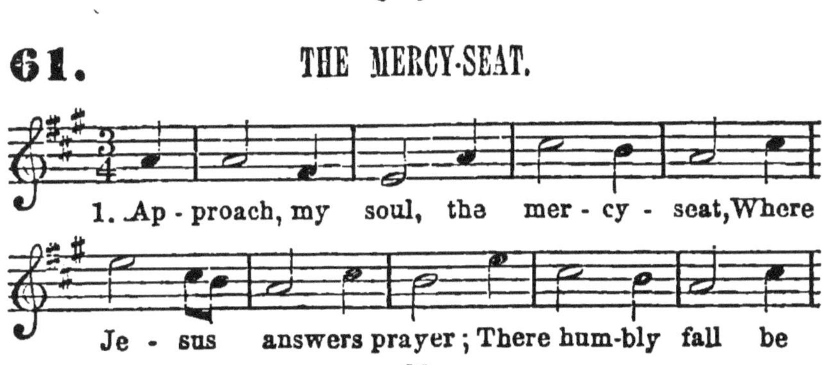
61. THE MERCY-SEAT.
1. Ap - proach, my soul, the mer - cy - seat, Where
Je - sus answers prayer; There hum-bly fall be

fore his feet, For none can per - ish there.

2. Thy promise is my only plea,
With this I venture nigh;
Thou callest burdened souls to thee,
And such, O Lord! am I.

3. Bowed down beneath a load of sin,
By Satan sorely pressed,
By wars without and fears within,
I come to thee for rest.

4. Be thou my shield and hiding-place,
That, sheltered near thy side,
I may my fierce accuser face,
And tell him thou hast died.

5. O wondrous love! to bleed and die,
To bear the cross and shame;
That guilty sinners such as I
Might plead thy gracious name!

62. LONG TIME AGO.

1. Je - sus died on Calvary's mountain, Long time a - go;
And sal -va-tion's roll-ing fountain Now free - ly flows.

2. Once his voice in tones of pity,
Melted in woe,
And he wept o 'er Judah's City,
Long time ago.

3. On his head the dews of midnight
Fell, long ago,
Now a crown of dazzling sunlight
Sits on his brow.

4. Jesus died—yet lives for ever,
No more to die—
Bleeding Jesus, Blessed Saviour,
Now reigns on high!

5. Now in heaven he 's interceding
For dying men,
Soon he 'll finish all his pleading,
And come again.

6. Budding fig-trees tell that summer
Dawns o 'er the land,
Signs portend that Jesus' coming,
Is near at hand.

7. Children, let your lights be burning,
In hope of heaven,
Waiting for our Lord's returning
At dawn or even.

8. When he comes, a voice from heaven
Shall pierce the tomb,
"Come, ye blessed of my Father,
Children, come home."

63. GLORY BE TO GOD.

1. Glo - ry be to God on high, God, whose
glo - ry fills the sky; Peace on earth, to

man for-given, Man, the well - be-loved of heaven.

2. Sov'reign Father, heavenly King,
Thee we now presume to sing;
Glad thine attributes confess,
Glorious all, and numberless.

3. Hail, by all thy works adored!
Hail, the everlasting Lord!
Thee with thankful hearts we prove,
God of power, and God of Love.

4. Christ our Lord and God we own,
Christ, the Father's only Son;
Lamb of God for sinners slain,
Saviour of offending man.

5. Jesus, in thy name we pray,
Take, O take our sins away;
Bow thine ear, in mercy bow.
Hear, the world's atonement, Thou!

6. Hear, for thou, O Christ, alone,
Art with thy great Father one;
One the Holy Ghost with thee;
One supreme eternal Three.

---

64. A LITTLE WHILE. *

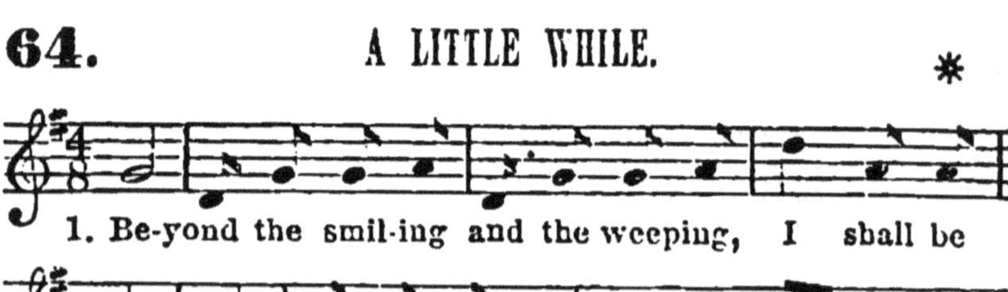
1. Be-yond the smil-ing and the weeping, I shall be
soon; Be - yond the wak-ing and the sleep - ing, Be-

A LITTLE WHILE. Concluded.

yond the sow-ing and the reap - ing, I shall be
Chorus.
soon. Love, rest, Love, rest, and home ! Sweet home !
Lord, tarry, tarry, tar - ry not, Lord, tarry not, but come.

2. Beyond the blooming and the fading,
I shall be soon;
Beyond the shining and the shading,
Beyond the hoping and the dreading,
I shall be soon, &c.

3. Beyond the rising and the setting,
I shall be soon;
Beyond the calming and the fretting,
Beyond remembering and forgetting,
I shall be soon, &c.

4. Beyond the parting and the meeting,
I shall be soon;
Beyond the farewell and the greeting,
Beyond the pulse's fever beating,
I shall be soon, &c.

5. Beyond the frost-chain and the fever,
I shall be soon;
Beyond the rock-waste and the river,
Beyond the ever and the never,
I shall be soon, &c.

65. THE GOSPEL FEAST.

1. Come, sin - ners, to the gos - pel feast, Let

ev - ery soul be Je - sus'
guest, You need not one be left be - hind, For
God hath bid - den all man - kind.

2. Sent by my Lord, on you I call:
The invitation is for all:
Come, all the world! come, sinner thou!
All things in Christ are ready now.

3. Come, all ye souls by sins oppressed,
Ye restless wanderers after rest;
Ye poor, and maimed, and halt, and blind,
In Christ a hearty welcome find,

4. My message as from God receive;
Ye all may come to Christ and live.
O let his love your hearts constrain,
Nor suffer him to die in vain.

5. This is the time, no more delay!
This is the Spirit's gracious day;
Come in this moment at his call,
And live for him who died for all.

66. FEAR NOT, LITTLE FLOCK.

1. { Glo - ry to God, that I have found The pearl of my sal -
I'm marching thro' Immanuel's ground, Up to my heavenly
D.S. Till I do o - ver -

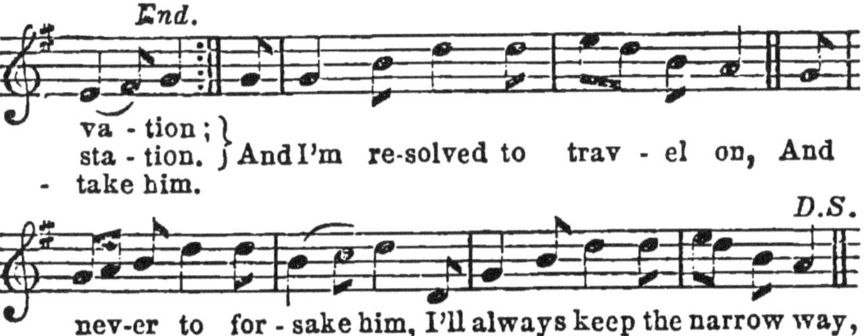
End.
va - tion;
sta - tion. And I'm re-solved to trav - el on, And
- take him.
D.S.
nev-er to for - sake him, I'll always keep the narrow way,

2. Fear not, says Christ, ye little flock,
   Heirs of immortal glory;
For ye are built upon the rock,
   The kingdom lies before you.
Fight on, fight on, ye heirs of grace,
   And tell the pleasing story;
I 'm with my little flock always,
   I 'll bring them home to glory.

---

67. WRESTLING JACOB

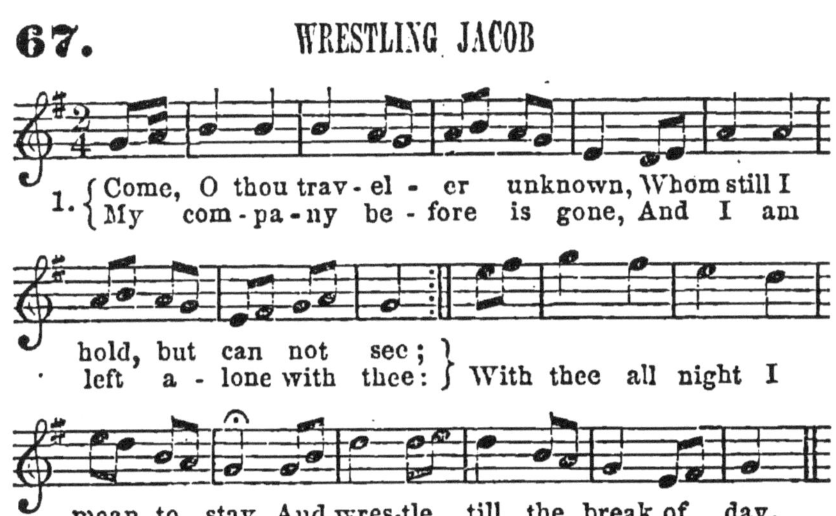
1. Come, O thou trav - el - er unknown, Whom still I
My com - pa - ny be - fore is gone, And I am
hold, but can not see;
left a - lone with thee: With thee all night I
mean to stay, And wres-tle till the break of day.

2. I need not tell thee who I am:
   My sin and misery declare;

Thyself hast called me by my name;
  Look on thy hands and read it there:
But who, I ask thee, who art thou?
Tell me thy name, and tell me now.

3. In vain thou strugglest to get free:
  I never will unloose my hold:
Art thou the Man that died for me?
  The secret of thy love unfold:
Wrestling, I will not let thee go,
Till I thy name, thy nature know.

4. Wilt thou not yet to me reveal
  Thy new, unutterable name?
Tell me, I beseech thee, tell;
  To know it now resolved I am.
Wrestling, I will not let thee go,
Till I thy name, thy nature know.

5. What, though my shrinking flesh complain,
  And murmur to contend so long?
I rise superior to my pain,
  When I am weak, then I am strong;
And when my all of strength shall fail,
I shall with the God-Man prevail.

68. THE PILGRIM'S REST.

1. There's a rest in yon - der sky, For my soul, For my
soul. There's a rest in yon - der sky, For my soul.
There's a rest in yon - der sky, And when I come to

THE PILGRIM'S REST. Concluded.

die, My ransomed soul shall fly To that rest, To that
rest, Then my ransomed soul shall fly To that rest.

2. Where sorrow's bitter stream
Never flows, &c.
But there love and joy abound,
Through Immanuel's happy ground,
And bright glory beams around,
Glorious rest, &c.

3. Though my trials are severe,
By the way, &c.
Though my trials are severe,
Yet my Saviour's always near,
And will guide me safely there,
To that rest, &c.

4. Sometimes the way seems hard,
To that rest, &c.
Sometimes the way seems hard,
But when I trust his word,
There I find that Christ the Lord
Gives me rest, &c.

5. Then, ye doubting souls, be strong
In the Lord, &c.
Then, ye doubting souls, be strong,
For your journey can't be long,
Soon you'll join the blood-washed throng,
In that rest, &c.

6. What a glorious time 't will be,
When at rest, &c.
When on heaven's peaceful plain
Parted friends shall meet again,
Far away from grief and pain,
Safe at rest, &c.

69. CAST YOUR DEADLY DOING DOWN.

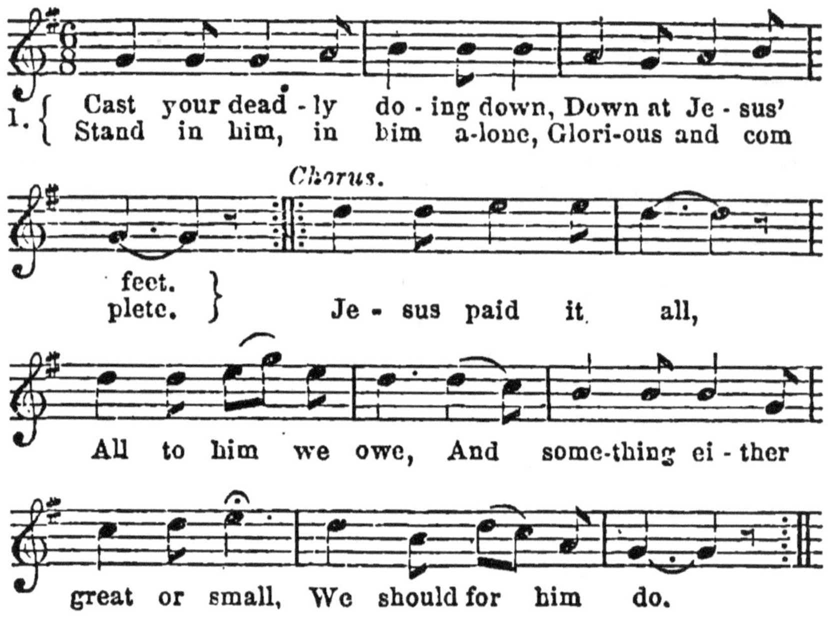

1. { Cast your dead - ly do - ing down, Down at Je - sus' feet.
Stand in him, in him a-lone, Glori-ous and com plete. }
Chorus.
Je - sus paid it all,
All to him we owe, And some-thing ei - ther
great or small, We should for him do.

2. You to Jesus' work should cling,
   By a simple faith,
   Doing is a deadly thing,
   It may be your death.—*Chorus.*

3. 'Twas for us that Jesus died,
   On the cruel tree;
   There he bowed his thorn-clad head,
   Oh! what agony!—*Chorus.*

4. 'Twas our sins that nailed him there,
   Ours that shed his blood,
   Ours that pierced the bleeding side
   Of the Son of God.—*Chorus.*

5. All your life should now be given
   To your risen Lord;
   Doing all the way to heaven
   Something in his word.—*Chorus.*

70. THE HOLY DAY.

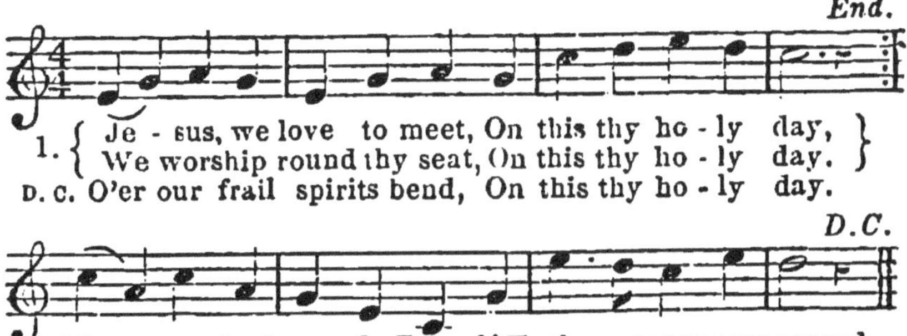
End.
1. { Je - sus, we love to meet, On this thy ho - ly day,
We worship round thy seat, On this thy ho - ly day. }
D. C. O'er our frail spirits bend, On this thy ho - ly day.
D.C.
Thou tender heavenly Friend! To thee our prayers ascend,

2. We dare not trifle now,
On this thy holy day.
In silent awe we bow,
On this thy holy day.
Check every wandering thought,
And let us all be taught,
To serve thee as we ought,
On this thy holy day.

3. We listen to thy word,
On this thy holy day.
Bless all that we have heard,
On this thy holy day.
Go with us when we part,
And to each longing heart,
Thy saving grace impart,
On this thy holy day.

---

71. THE GARDEN HYMN.

1. The Lord in - to his gar-den comes; The spi-ces yield a

rich perfume, The lilies glow and thrive; The li-lies grow and

thrive: Refreshing showers of grace divine, From Jesus flow to

every vine, Which makes the dead revive, Which makes the dead, &c

2. Oh, that this dry and barren ground
In springs of water may abound,
A fruitful soil become!
The desert blossoms as the rose,
When Jesus conquers all his foes,
And makes his people one.

3. The glorious time is rolling on,
The gracious work is now begun,
My soul a witness is:
I taste and see the pardon free,
For all mankind as well as me,
Who come to Christ may live.

4. We feel that heaven is now begun,
It issues from a shining throne,
From Jesus' throne on high;
It comes like floods we can't contain;
We drink, and drink, and drink again,
And yet we still are dry.

5. But when we come to reign above,
And all surround the throne of love,
We'll drink a full supply;
Jesus will lead his armies through
To living fountains where they flow,
That never will run dry.

6. There we shall reign, and shout, and sing,
And make the upper regions ring,
When all the saints get home:

Come on, come on, my brethren dear,
Soon we shall meet together there,
For Jesus bids us come.

7. Amen, Amen, my soul replies,
I'm bound to meet you in the skies,
And claim my mansion there:
Now here's my heart, and here's my hand,
To meet you in that heavenly land,
Where we shall part no more.

72. GOD IS LOVE. S. T. E. *

1. Come let us all u - nite and sing, God is
love. While heaven and earth their prais - es bring,
God is love. Let eve - ry soul from
sin awake, Their harps now from the willows take, And
sing with me for Je - sus' sake, God is love.

2. Oh! tell to earth's remotest bound,
God is love.
In Christ I have redemption found;
God is love.
His blood has washed my sins away;

His Spirit turns my night to day;
And now my soul with joy can say,
God is love.

3. How happy is our portion here;
God is love.
His promises our spirits cheer;
God is love.
He is our sun and shield by day,
By night He near our tents will stay,
He will be with us all the way,
God is love.

4. What though my heart and flesh shall fail,
God is love.
Through Christ I shall o'er death prevail,
God is love.
Through Jordan's swell I will not fear;
My Jesus will be with me there,
My head above the waves to bear,
God is love.

73. WE'RE TRAVELING HOME.

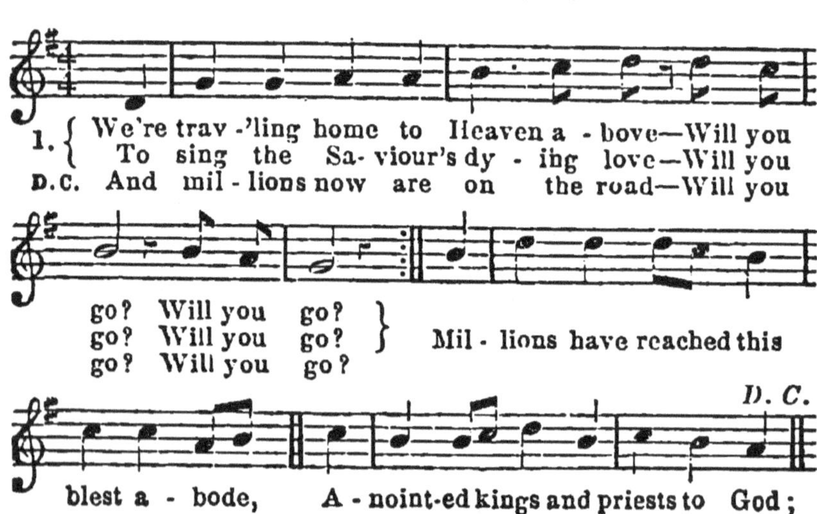
1. { We're trav-'ling home to Heaven a-bove—Will you go? Will you go?
To sing the Sa-viour's dy-ing love—Will you go? Will you go? }
D.C. And mil-lions now are on the road—Will you go? Will you go?
Mil-lions have reached this blest a-bode,
A-noint-ed kings and priests to God;
D. C.

2. We're going to see the bleeding Lamb,
Will you go?
In rapturous strains to praise his name,
Will you go?
The crown of life we there shall wear,
The conqueror's palms our hands shall bear,
And all the joys of heaven we'll share,
Will you go?

3. We're going to join the Heavenly Choir,
Will you go?
To raise our voice and tune the lyre,
Will you go?
The saints and angels gladly sing,
Hosanna to their God and King.
And make the heavenly arches ring,
Will you go?

4. Ye weary, heavy-laden, come,
Will you go?
In the blest house there still is room,
Will you go?
The Lord is waiting to receive,
If thou wilt on him now believe,
He'll give thy troubled conscience ease,
Come believe!

5. The way to Heaven is free for all,
Will you go?
For Jews and Gentiles, great and small,
Will you go?
Make up your mind, Give God your heart,
With every sin and idol part,
And now for glory make a start,
Come away!

6. The way to Heaven is straight and plain,
Will you go?
Repent, believe, be born again,
Will you go?

The Saviour cries aloud to thee,
"Take up thy cross and follow me,"
And thou shalt my salvation see,
Come to me!

7. Oh, could I hear some sinner say,
I will go!
I'll start this moment, clear the way,
Let me go!
My old companions, fare you well,
I will not go with you to hell!
I mean with Jesus Christ to dwell,
Let me go! Fare you well.

74. HE'S THE LILY OF THE VALLEY.

Chorus.
He's the li - ly of the val - ly
End.
Oh my Lord! Oh my Lord! I I tell you what I
mean to do, Oh my Lord! I mean to go to
hea - ven too, Oh my Lord.
D.C.

2. I'm going away to leave you,
Oh, my Lord!
Oh, sin no more, I pray you,
Oh, my Lord.—*Chorus.*

3. I do believe, without a doubt,
Oh, my Lord!
The Christian has a right to shout,
Oh, my Lord!—*Chorus.*

4. My duty makes me understand,
Oh, my Lord!
That we must take the parting hand,
Oh, my Lord!—*Chorus.*

75. THE GOSPEL VOYAGE.

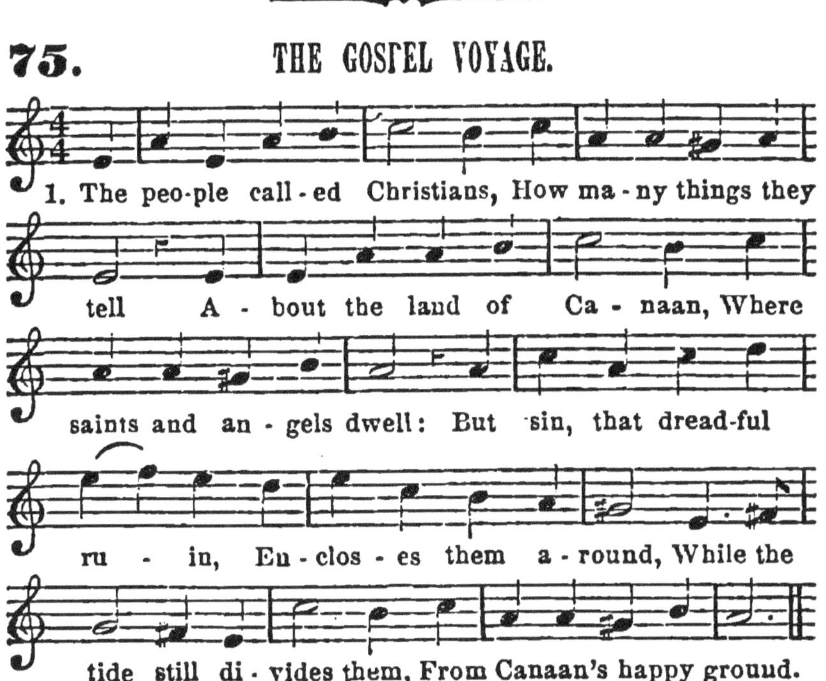
1. The peo-ple call-ed Christians, How ma-ny things they
tell A-bout the land of Ca-naan, Where
saints and an-gels dwell: But sin, that dread-ful
ru-in, En-clos-es them a-round, While the
tide still di-vides them, From Canaan's happy ground.

2. Thousands have been impatient
To find a passage through,
And, with united vigor,
Have tried what they could do;
But vessels built by human skill,
Have never sailed afar,
Till they found them aground,
On some dreadful sandy bar.

3. The everlasting gospel
   Has launched the deep at last,
Behold her sails extended,
   Around her towering masts;
Along her deck, in order,
   Her joyful sailors stand,
Crying, "Ho! here we go
   To Immanuel's happy land."

4. To those who are spectators,
   What anguish must ensue,
To hear their old companions
   Bid them a long adieu!
The pleasures of a paradise
   No longer them invite;
They may rail while we sail,
   But we'll soon be out of sight.

5. We're now on the wide ocean,
   We bid the world farewell;
But where we shall cast anchor
   No human tongue can tell;
About our future happiness
   There need be no debate,
While we ride on the tide,
   With our captain and his mate.

6. The passengers united
   In order, peace, and love,
The wind all in our favor,
   How sweetly we do move;
Though troubles may surround us,
   And raging billows roar,
We will keep on the deep,
   Till we land on Canaan's shore.

76. ROLL ON.

1. Soon will our weep - ing time be o'er, When we shall

Chorus.
weep and sigh no more. Roll on, roll on, sweet
moments, roll on, And let these poor pilgrims go home, go home.

2. Jesus himself shall guide our way,
Till safe we rest in endless day.

3. A few more rolling years at most,
Will land us safe on Canaan's coast.

4. From sleeping clay and beds of dust,
Our Jesus will call home the just.

5. Our ransomed souls shall soar away,
To praise our God in endless day.

6. When landed on the heavenly shore,
Death and the curse shall be no more.

7. And when we Christ in glory meet,
Our thrilling hopes will be complete.

8. Then shall we sing the song of grace,
Safe in our glorious dwelling place.

77. ON THE ROAD TO HEAVEN, *

1. I'm on the road to hea - ven now, Don't
grieve af - ter me, I'm on the road to hea-ven now, Don't

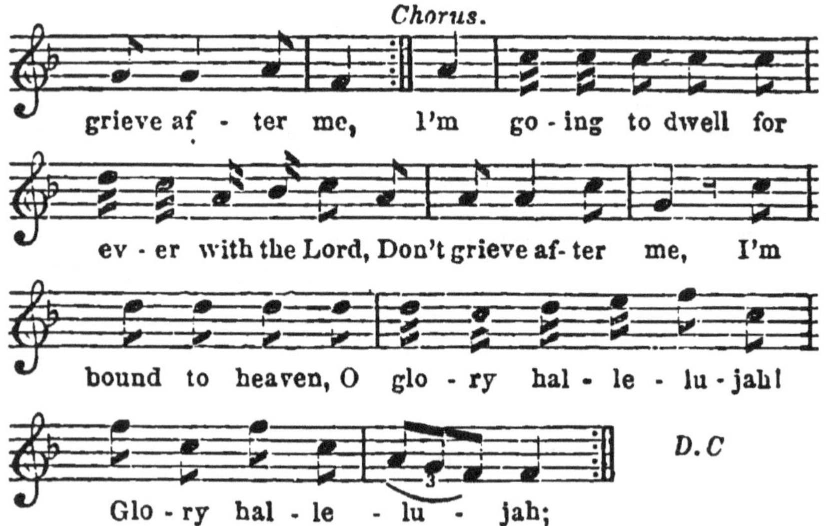
Chorus.
grieve af - ter me, I'm go - ing to dwell for
ev - er with the Lord, Don't grieve af- ter me, I'm
bound to heaven, O glo - ry hal - le - lu - jah!
Glo - ry hal - le - lu - jah;
D.C

2. The road to glory's through the sea,
   Don't grieve after me;
   But my Lord Jesus will guide me,
   Don't grieve after me.—*Chorus.*

3. I've left all that this world can give,
   Don't grieve after me;
   I live for Christ, and die to live,
   Don't grieve after me.—*Chorus.*

4. Oh, why, dear friends, do you lament!
   Don't grieve after me;
   But meet me at the Great Judgment
   Of all, on the last day.—*Chorus.*

78. MARCHING TO GLORY.

{ Our kindred dear to heav'n are gone, We'll meet our friends in
{ They lan-ded safe we'll fol-low on To meet our friends in
D. C. We're on our way to par - a -dise, To meet our friends in

End. Chorus.
glo - ry,
glo - ry;
glo - ry.
We're march-ing to glo - ry, We're
march - ing to glo - ry, We're marching to
glo - ry, To meet our friends in glo - ry.
D.C.

2. They had to fight their passage through,
We'll meet, &c.
But conquered, as we soon shall do.

3. Now they are shining bright and fair, &c.
Victorious palms with joy they bear.

4. Safe housed in their eternal home, &c.
They wait till we with songs shall come.

5. How happy they from sorrow free, &c.
And such our happiness shall be—

6. How bright the crown their temples bear, &c.
Like crowns for us are waiting there—

79. OH! LOOK! *

Chorus.
1. Oh look! Oh look! Oh look?
End.
Look at the Lord stand - ing at the door!

OH! LOOK! Concluded.

Bands of an-gels af-ter me, Oh look!
Oh look! I shall soon in
hea-ven be, Oh look! Oh look!
D.C.

2. Jesus knocks, has knocked before,
O look! O look!
For to be saved, open the door,
O look! O look!—*Chorus.*

3. Sinner, let Lord Jesus in,
O look! O look!
He will cleanse you from all sin,
O look! O look!—*Chorus.*

80. OH! WHO'S LIKE JESUS.

1. { Je-sus my all to heaven is gone: He
His track I see and I'll pur-sue The
1st.
whom I fix my hopes up-on:
nar-row way, till - - - - - - - - him I view.
Chorus.
Oh! whose like Je-sus who died on the tree? ? He

OH! WHO'S LIKE JESUS? Concluded.

died for you, he died for me, He
died to set poor sin - ners free, Oh! who's like
Je - sus who died on the tree?

2. The way the holy prophets went
The road that leads from banishment:
The King's highway of truth I'll go,
For all his paths are peace and joy.

3. This is the way I long have sought,
And mourned because I found it not;
My grief and burden long has been,
Because I was not saved from sin.—*Chorus.*

4. The more I strove against its power,
I felt its weight and guilt the more;
Till late I heard my Saviour say:
"Come hither, soul, I AM THE WAY."—*Chorus.*

5. Lo! glad I come, and thou, blest Lamb,
Shalt take me to thee, whose I am;
Nothing but sin have I to give,
Nothing but love shall I receive.—*Chorus.*

6. Then will I tell to sinners round,
What a dear Saviour I have found;
I'll point to thy redeeming blood,
And say, "Behold thy way to God."—*Chorus.*

---

81. THE UNION BAND.

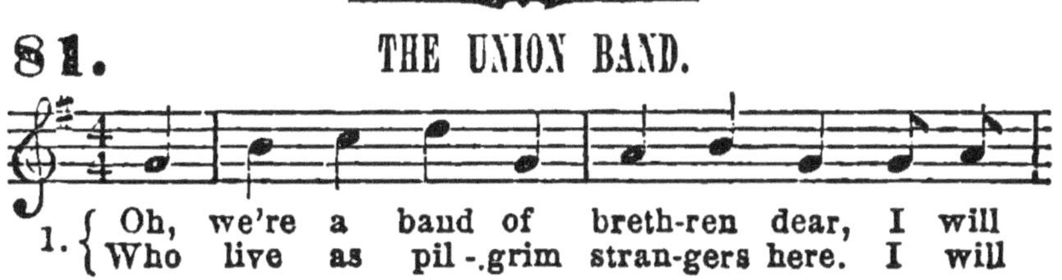
1. { Oh, we're a band of breth-ren dear, I will
Who live as pil-.grim stran-gers here. I will

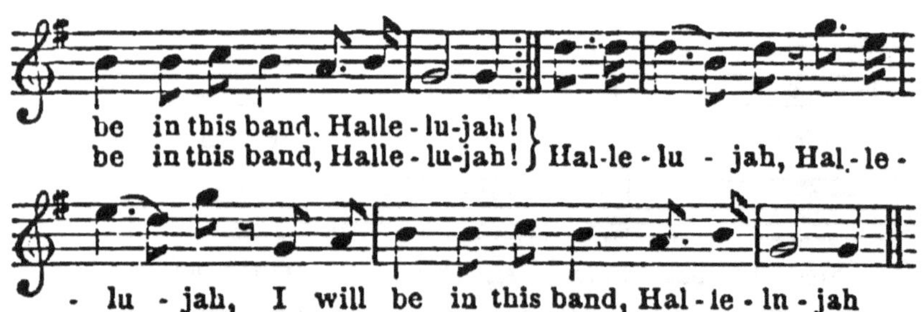
be in this band. Halle - lu-jah! }
be in this band, Halle - lu-jah! } Hal-le - lu - jah, Hal.- le -
- lu - jah, I will be in this band, Hal - le - lu - jah

2. The prophets and apostles, too,
All belonged to this band, &c.
And all God's children here below,
I will be in this band, &c.

3. We're travelling home to heaven above, I will, &c.
To sing the Saviour's dying love. I will, &c.

4. The crown of life we there shall wear, I will, &c.
The conqueror's palm our hands shall bear, I will, &c.

5. Oh, glorious hope—oh, blest abode, I will, &c.
We shall be near and like our Lord, I will, &c.

6. A little longer here below, I will, &c.
Then home to glory we shall go, I will, &c.

7. Come on, come on, my brethren dear, I will &c.
We soon shall meet together there. I will, &c

82. PISGAH.

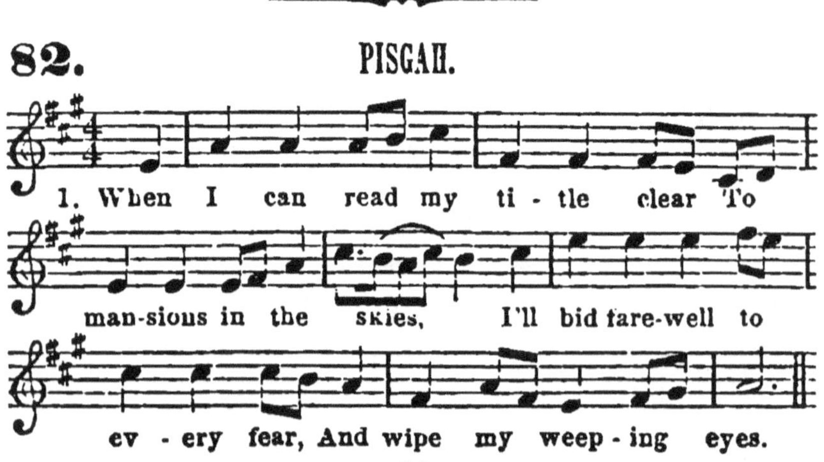
1. When I can read my ti - tle clear To
man-sions in the skies, I'll bid fare-well to
ev - ery fear, And wipe my weep - ing eyes.

2. Should earth against my soul engage,
And fiery darts be hurled,
Then I can smile at Satan's rage,
And face a frowning world.

3. Let cares like a wild deluge come,
Let storms of sorrow fall;
So I but safely reach my home,
My God, my heaven, my all.

4. Then shall I bathe my weary soul
In seas of heavenly rest,
And not a wave of trouble roll
Across my peaceful breast.

83. MOURNING PILGRIM.

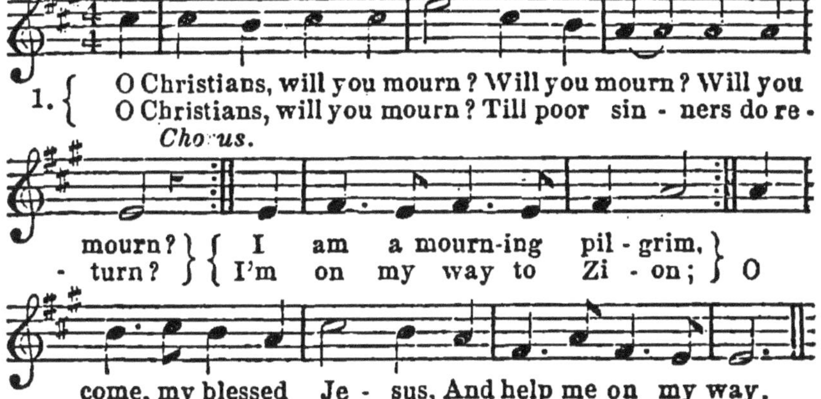
1. { O Christians, will you mourn? Will you mourn? Will you mourn? }
{ O Christians, will you mourn? Till poor sin - ners do re - turn? }
Chorus.
{ I am a mourn-ing pil - grim, }
{ I'm on my way to Zi - on; } O
come, my blessed Je - sus, And help me on my way.

2. O brethren, will you mourn, &c., &c.
Till your children do return?—*Chorus.*

3. O sinners, you will mourn, &c., &c.
If to Christ you ne'er return.

Chorus.—Then haste and join our number,
And go with us to Zion:
O come, my blessed Jesus,
And help us on our way.

REST FOR THE WEARY.

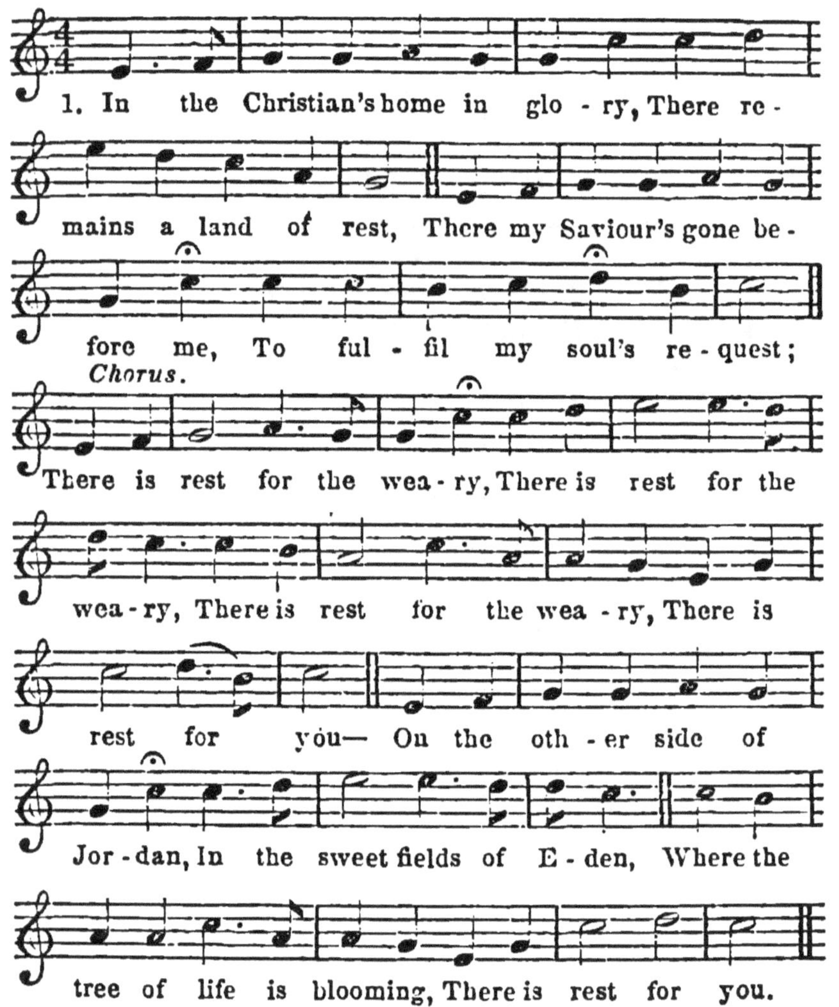
1. In the Christian's home in glo - ry, There re -
mains a land of rest, There my Saviour's gone be -
fore me, To ful - fil my soul's re - quest;
Chorus.
There is rest for the wea - ry, There is rest for the
wea - ry, There is rest for the wea - ry, There is
rest for you— On the oth - er side of
Jor - dan, In the sweet fields of E - den, Where the
tree of life is blooming, There is rest for you.

2. He is fitting up my mansion,
   Which eternally shall stand,
For my stay shall not be transient,
   In that holy, happy land.—*Chorus*

3. Pain and sickness ne'er shall enter,
   Grief nor woe my lot shall share,
But in that celestial centre,
   I a crown of life shall wear.—*Chorus.*

4. Sing, O sing, ye heirs of glory;
Shout your triumphs as you go;
Zion's gates will open for you,
You shall find an entrance thro'.—*Chorus.*

85. WE'LL STEM THE STORM.

1. A - rise my soul, to Pis - gah's height, And
Chorus.
We'll stem the storm, it won't be long, The

view the prom-ised land, And see by faith the
heaven - ly port is nigh; We'll stem the storm it

glori - ous sight, Our her - it - age at hand.
won't be long, We'll an - chor by - and - by.

2. Fair Salem's dazzling gates are seen,
Just o'er the narrow flood,
And fields adorned in living green,
The residence of God. *Chorus.*

3. O could I cross rough Jordan's wave,
No danger would I fear;
My bark would every tempest brave,
For O! my Captain's near. *Chorus.*

4. My lamp of life will soon grow pale,
The spark will soon decay;
And then my happy soul will sail
To everlasting day. *Chorus.*

86. WE'RE GOING HOME.

1. We go the way that leads to God, The
CHOR. We're go - ing home, we're go - ing home, We're

way that saints have ev - er trod; So let us leave this
go - ing home, to die no more, To die no more, to

sin - ful shore, For realms where we shall die no more.
die no more, We're go - ing home to die no more.

2. The ways of God are ways of bliss,
And all his paths are happiness;
Then, weary souls, your sighs give o'er,
We're going home, to die no more.—*Chorus.*

3. There is a land beyond the sky,
Where happy spirits never sigh;
Then, erring souls, your sins deplore,
And sing of where we'll die no more.—*Chorus.*

4. Come, sinners, come, O come along.
And join our happy pilgrim throng;
Farewell, vain world, and all your store;
We're going home, to die no more.—*Chorus.*

---

87. GIVE ME JESUS.

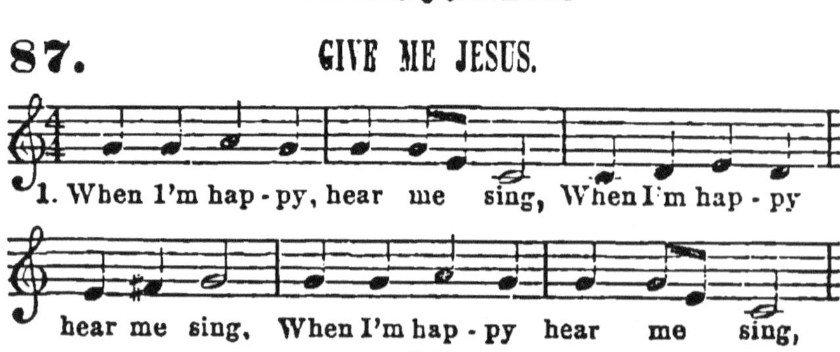
1. When I'm hap - py, hear me sing, When I'm hap - py
hear me sing, When I'm hap - py hear me sing,

Give me Je - sus, Give me Je sus, Give me Je
sus : You may have all the world : Give me Je - sus

2. When in sorrow, hear me pray, &c. *Chorus.*

3. When I 'm dying, hear me cry, &c. *Chorus.*

4. When I 'm rising, hear me shout, &c.
I have Jesus, I have Jesus, I have Jesus, &c.

5. When in heaven, we will sing, &c.
Blessed Jesus, blessed Jesus, blessed Jesus,
By thy grace we are saved, blessed Jesus.

88. THE YOUNG CONVERT.

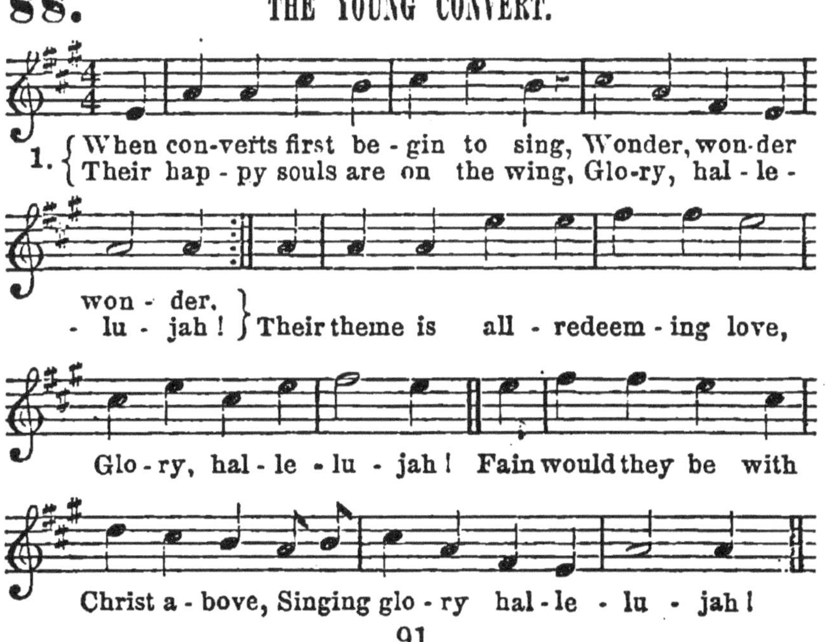
1. { When con-verts first be - gin to sing, Wonder, won-der won - der.
Their hap - py souls are on the wing, Glo-ry, hal - le - - lu - jah ! } Their theme is all - redeem - ing love,
Glo - ry, hal - le - lu - jah ! Fain would they be with
Christ a - bove, Singing glo - ry hal - le - lu - jah !

2. With admiration they behold, Wonder, &c.
The love of Christ that can't be told, Glory, &c.
They view themselves upon the shore, &c.
And think the battle all is o'er, &c.

3. They feel themselves quite free from pain,
And think their enemies are slain;
They make no doubt but all is well,
And Satan is cast down to hell.

4. They wonder why old saints do n't sing,
And make the heavenly arches ring;
Ring with melodious, joyful sound,
Because a prodigal is found.

5. Come, take up arms and face the field.
Come, gird on harness, sword and shield;
Stand fast in faith, fight for your King,
And soon the victory you shall win.

6. When Satan comes to tempt your minds,
Then meet him with these blessed lines—
For Christ our Lord has swept the field,
And we 're determined not to yield.

89. REST IN HEAVEN.

1. My rest is in heaven, my rest is not here;
Then why should I murmur at tri-als severe?
Be tranquil, my spi-rit, the worst that can come,

But shortens my journey, and hastens me home.

2. It is not for me to be seeking my bliss,
And staying my hopes in a region like this;
I look for a city not builded with hands,
And its glorious temple eternally stands.

3. Afflictions may try me—they cannot destroy;
One vision of home turns them all into joy;
And the bitterest tears that flow from mine eyes,
But sweeten my hope of that home in the skies.

4. Let trouble and danger my progress oppose;
They can only make heav'n more bright at the close:
Come joy, or come sorrow, whate'er may befall,
One moment in glory will make up for all.

5. A scrip on my back, and a staff in my hand,
I march on in haste through an enemy's land;
The road may be rough, but it cannot be long,
And I'll smooth it with hope, and cheer it with song.

90. THE HEAVENLY HOST.

1. Who are these in bright ar - ray, This ex - ult - ing,

hap - py throng, Round the al - tar night and day,

Hymning one tri - umphant song? "Worthy is the

Lamb once slain, Bless-ing, hon - or, glo - ry, power,
Wis - dom, rich - es to ob - tain,
New do - min - ion ev - ery hour.

2. These through fiery trials trod;
   These from great afflictions came;
Now before the throne of God,
   Sealed with his almighty name:
Clad in raiment pure and white,
   Victor-palms in every hand:
Through their great Redeemer's might,
   More than conquerors they stand.

3. Hunger, thirst, disease, unknown,
   On immortal fruits they feed:
Them the Lamb, amidst the throne,
   Shall to living fountains lead:
Joy and gladness banish sighs:
   Perfect love dispels all fears;
And for ever from their eyes
   God shall wipe away their tears.

CONTENTS,

CONTENTS.

www.ingramcontent.com/pod-product-compliance
Lightning Source LLC
Chambersburg PA
CBHW031439270326
41930CB00007B/791

* 9 7 8 3 3 3 7 4 0 4 6 5 9 *